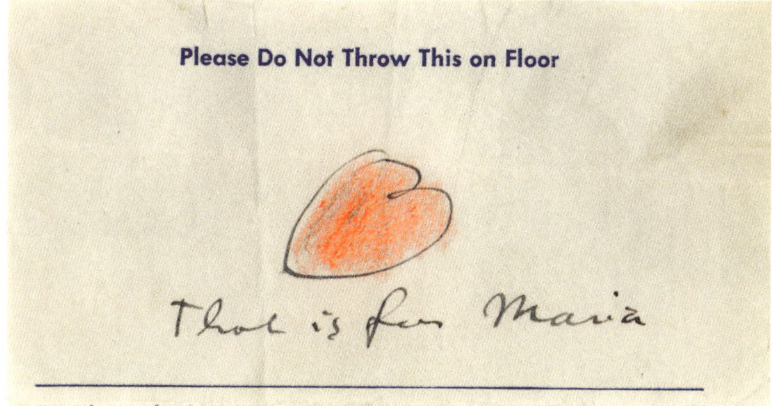
Please Do Not Throw This on Floor

Impossible

Francis M. Naumann

Impossible

The Love Affair between Marcel Duchamp & Maria Martins and the Artwork It Inspired

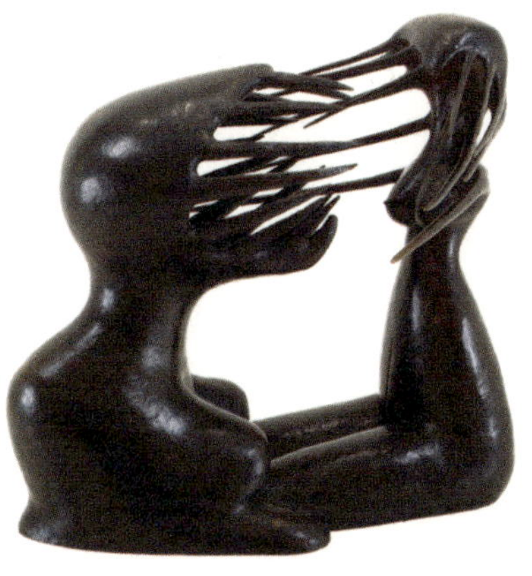

Abbeville Press

NEW YORK   LONDON

"It's fun to read and a real contribution to the ever-widening literature on Duchamp. Naumann makes its central characters—Marcel and Maria—both come alive on the page."

—*Calvin Tomkins, staff writer for The New Yorker
and author of* Duchamp: A Biography

"This book provides a fascinating account of one of modern art's greatest love stories. Beautifully written and informed by meticulous research, Francis M. Naumann has given us an instant classic: a must-read for anyone interested in human creativity and its inspirations."

—*Michael R. Taylor, Chief Curator and Deputy
Director, Virginia Museum of Fine Arts*

"Fascinating! Naumann offers new insights into the relationship between Marcel Duchamp and Maria Martins, a romance that resulted in the creation of entirely new works by each artist. He shows how a passionate woman from the tropics influenced the heart and mind of one of the greatest intellects of modern times. Naumann's writing is so fresh and immediate that it creates a sensation of the reader being there, a voyeur witnessing one of the most fertile, yet impossible erotic encounters to have taken place between two artists in the history of twentieth century art."

—*Graça Ramos, PhD, Brazilian journalist and
author of* Maria Martins: Escultora dos Trópicos

Front endpaper illustration: See Fig. 53.
Title page illustration: See Fig. 23.

Design: Misha Beletsky
Cover concept: Francis M. Naumann, Marie T. Keller,
and David Fabricant

For works by Maria Martins: © Estate of
María Martins / SPA, Lisbon / Licensed by VAGA at Artists
Rights Society (ARS), New York.

For works by Marcel Duchamp:
© Association Marcel Duchamp, Artists Rights Society (ARS),
New York / ADAGP, Paris.

First edition
10 9 8 7 6 5 4 3 2 1

ISBN 978-0-7892-1529-1

Library of Congress Cataloging-in-Publication Data
available upon request

For bulk and premium sales and for text adoption procedures,
write to Customer Service Manager, Abbeville Press, 655 Third
Avenue, New York, NY 10017, or call 1-800-ARTBOOK.

Visit Abbeville Press online at www.abbeville.com.

For Terry, whom I love with my whole heart

CONTENTS

INTRODUCTION

ell me who your enemies are, so that I can help you to hate them." Those were likely the first words spoken by the Brazilian sculptor Maria Martins to Marcel Duchamp when she introduced herself to him at an art opening in 1943.

It is hard to know how the French artist would have reacted to such an aggressive greeting, for whenever he met someone for the first time, what that person said was usually more polite and genteel. After all, at age fifty-six, Duchamp was long regarded as a venerated figure in the art world, famous for having submitted the painting of a descending nude at the Armory Show thirty years earlier and, shortly thereafter, for having abandoned fame and fortune in the world of art to devote himself to playing chess. Maria Martins was seven years his junior and married to the Brazilian ambassador to the United States, although it is uncertain how much Duchamp knew about her private life at the time they met. The artist's principal biographer would later describe Maria as "a small, dark-haired, vibrantly attractive woman," which photographs of her from this period confirm, but they reveal little of the colorful and

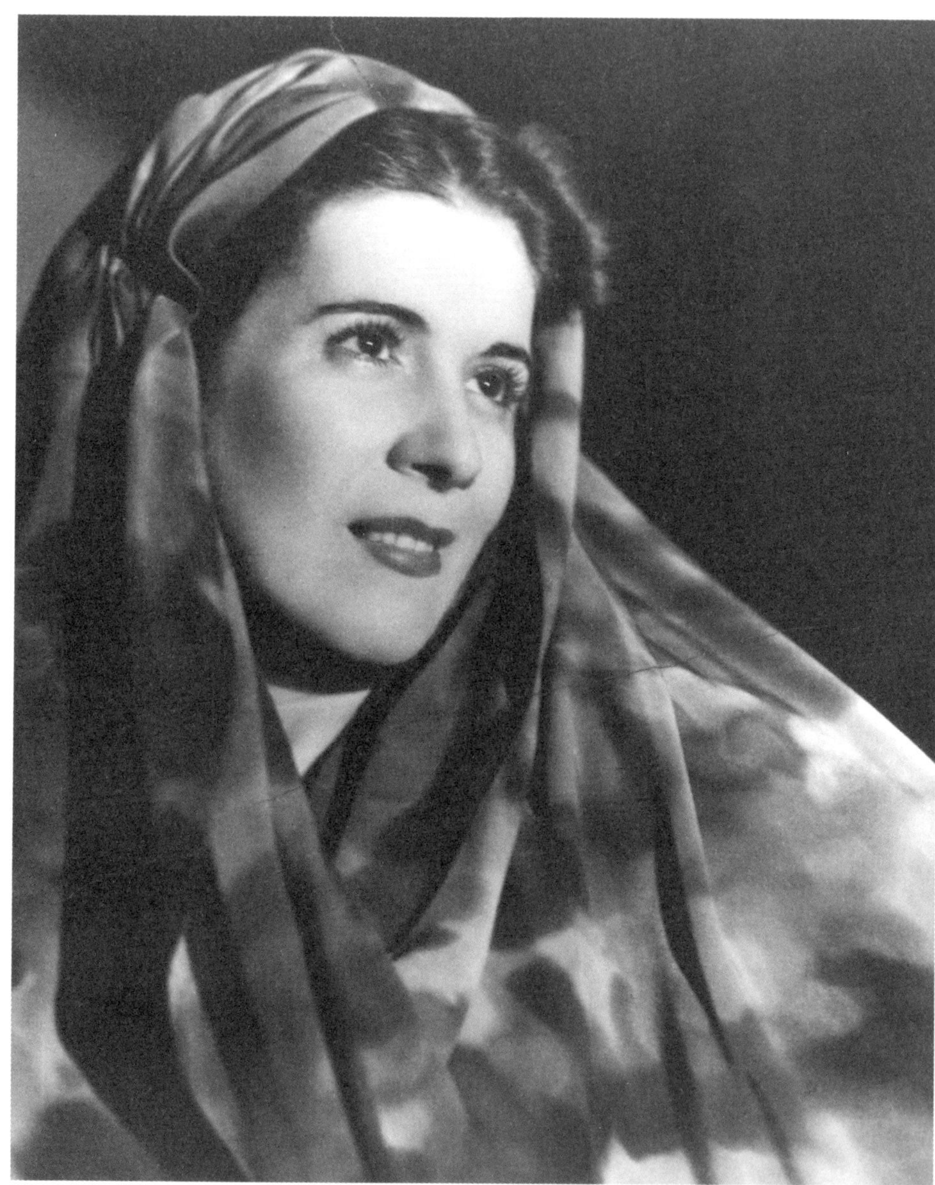

Fig. 1. Maria Martins, 1941. Unknown photographer. Formerly
collection Nora Lobo, São Paulo.

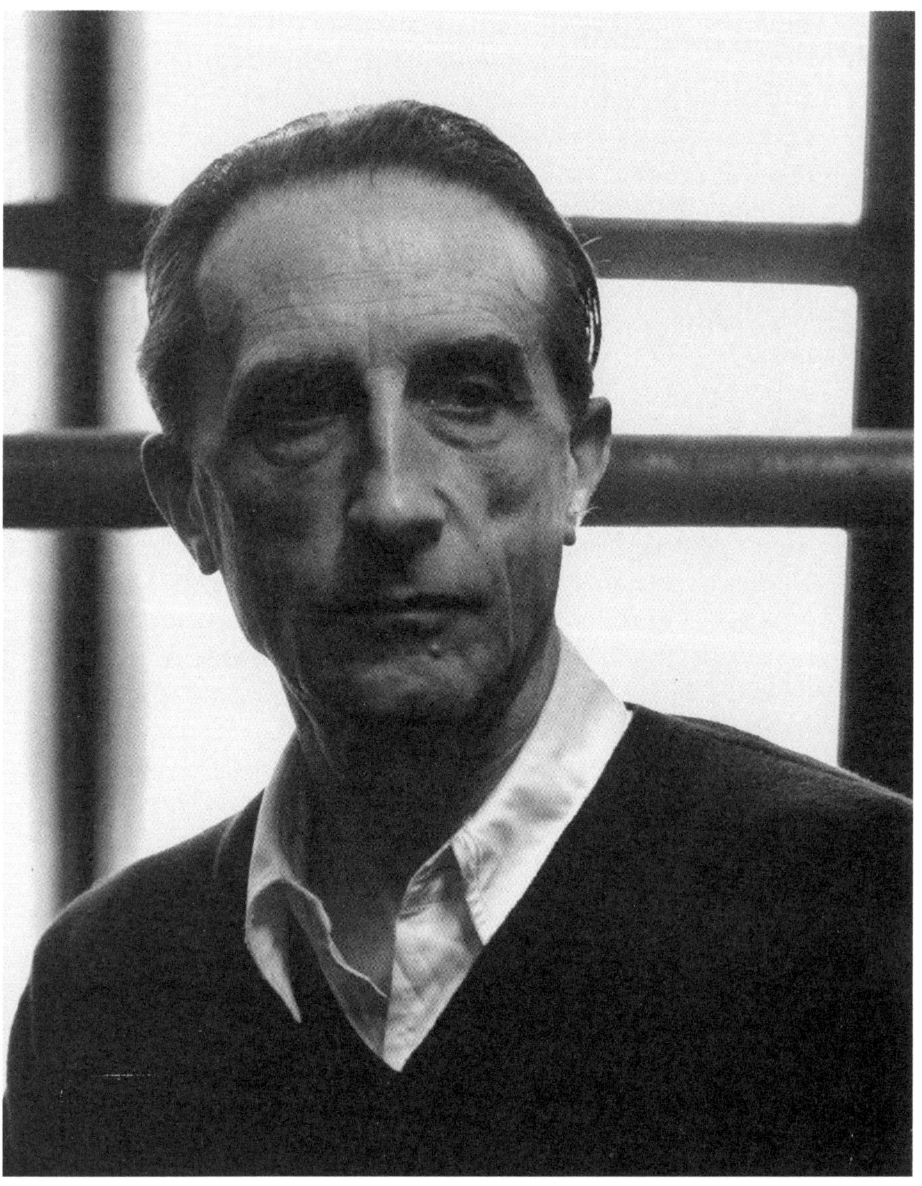

Fig. 2. Marcel Duchamp in his 14th Street Studio, 1949. Photograph by Naomi Savage. Collection Francis M. Naumann and Marie T. Keller, Yorktown Heights, New York.

explosive personality that attracted Duchamp; she was forthright and raw, a woman who held nothing back and made it clear how she felt about someone from the moment she met them. He did not realize it at the time, but this woman would go on to become the center of his emotional life for the next seven to eight years, a relationship that would reach a dramatic crescendo in 1946–47, but which would be the main focus of his creative activities—the majority of which were conducted in secrecy—for some twenty years to come.

Marcel and Maria came from very different cultural backgrounds, but there were curious similarities in their upbringing. They were both born and raised in fairly small towns, but as their fathers advanced in their respective professions—Maria's was a lawyer, Duchamp's a notary—they moved to larger cities nearby. Maria was enrolled in a French Catholic school outside of Rio de Janeiro, where she learned to speak French fluently, whereas Duchamp attended a boarding school in Rouen. Maria was instinctively defiant and quarreled with her mother, whereas Duchamp got along well with his parents, but did not fully accept the rules imposed on him by his school or by the church. Both he and Maria were brought up Catholic. The main difference in their upbringing was that Duchamp came from a family of artists, his two older brothers already well established by the time he set out to join them in Paris. Maria had two younger sisters, but no one in the family professed any interest in the arts. She studied the piano and classical music as a child and had aspirations of becoming a concert conductor, but extreme nervousness during a public performance caused her to abandon such lofty ambitions. Her father instilled in her a love for classical literature, reading to her as a child the writings of Goethe and Dante, and as she later wrote, "He left me this indomitable passion for the works of the spirit: *Art, Poetry, Philosophy*." Marcel also loved and admired his father; for a while, he even thought of following in his footsteps and becoming a notary.

Both Marcel and Maria were brought up in comparative comfort, privileged backgrounds that made it possible for them to think about their future as more than a quest for employment to support themselves, and they were free to choose the career path of their liking. She would eventually go on to become a noted sculptor, a vocation that she only began to pursue comparatively late in life, in her early forties, and then only after having been married twice and giving birth to five daughters. Duchamp would follow the lead of his older brothers and become an artist, not a painter or sculptor like them, but a profound intellect who challenged all forms of conventional art. After spending some years as a painter, he would come up with an entirely new concept of art, one that changed the very definition of art as it had become traditionally known and understood.

MEETING

It is not really known exactly when Marcel and Maria met, but it was likely on March 22, 1943, at the opening of Martins's second show of sculpture at the Valentine Gallery on East 57th Street in New York, which was held in conjunction with an exhibition of new paintings by Piet Mondrian. From photographs of both artists that survive from this period (Figs. 1 and 2), it is easy to see what attracted them physically to each other. She had smooth porcelain skin, black hair, defined eyebrows, sharply drawn lips, and dark penetrating eyes, features that most men found irresistible, whereas Duchamp was habitually thin and enduringly handsome, spoke with slow thoughtful pauses, and as many who knew him later reported, moved his hands with the grace of a ballet dancer. Their temperaments were, however, anything but similar, as she was instinctively impulsive, direct, and decisive, while Duchamp was by nature an introvert; he avoided conflict, choosing to gently remove himself from any unpleasant situation rather than become involved. Whereas Maria was quick to warmly embrace any relationship that came along, he was more reticent, never allowing himself to become emotionally attached to anyone, especially the women who came into his life.

Duchamp would have attended the opening at the Valentine Gallery at the behest of Mondrian, as he had known the Dutch artist from his years in Paris and had helped place examples of his work into important collections in the United States. Mondrian fled from Paris to London in 1938 and, in 1940, moved to New York, where he would remain for the last four years of his life. (He died in 1944, at the age of seventy-one.) What was on display by Maria in the gallery that night might have taken Duchamp by surprise, as it had nothing to do with the rigidly abstract paintings of Mondrian, but rather consisted of sculptures that were highly emotive depictions of figures drawn from Brazilian folk legend. The show was accompanied by a lavish portfolio publication called *Amazonia* (Fig. 3), featuring on its cover an overhead map of the Amazon River, colored blood red and placed against an emerald-green ground. Maria gave copies of this publication to many of her guests attending the opening, and there is no reason to believe that she would not have given one to Duchamp. Nothing is known of what he and Maria talked about at the opening, but there was enough said to warrant another meeting, which likely took place at her studio around the corner from the Valentine Gallery a few weeks after the opening.

Between their first meeting and the next, Duchamp had several opportunities to learn more about the woman he just met. A few weeks after the opening, *Vogue* magazine published an article about Maria meant to coincide with her exhibition. There Duchamp would have learned that she was the wife of the Brazilian

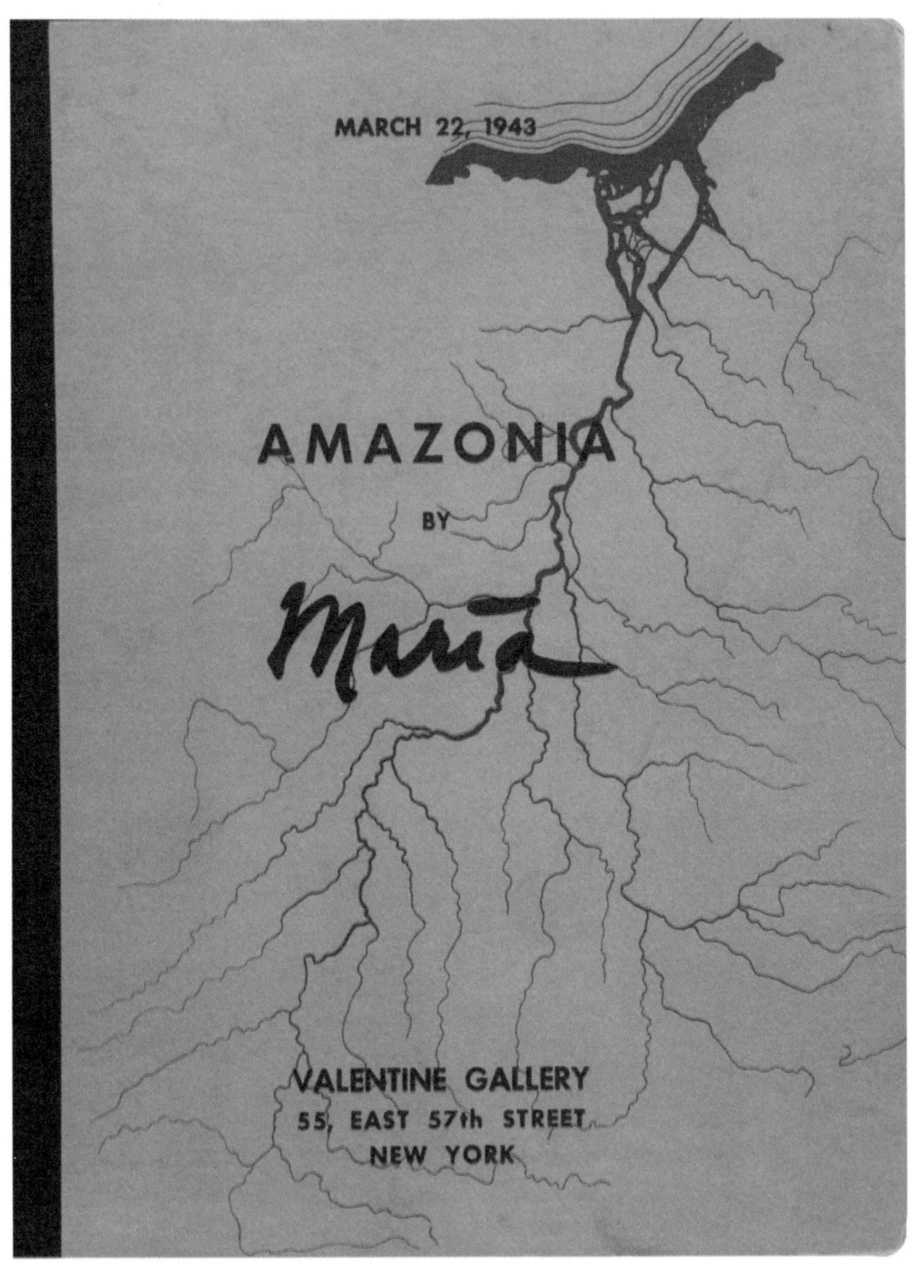

Fig. 3. Maria Martins, *Amazonia*, 1943. Cover to Martins's portfolio published in conjunction with an exhibition at the Valentine Gallery, New York; collection Francis M. Naumann, New York.

ambassador to the United States, and that she had three daughters. A full-page photograph shows the artist carving a life-size female figure (Fig. 4), as the sculpture of a nude woman with upraised hands stands directly behind her. The sculpture was one of many, the author explained, that filled her studio in the attic of the embassy in Washington, DC. Whereas the article did focus on her social responsibilities as the wife of the ambassador, it also mentioned that she had assembled an impressive collection of rare jades and porcelains, African masks, and Persian pottery, as well as paintings by Renoir, Degas, Léger, Soutine, and Chagall. It concluded by mentioning her show at the Valentine Gallery, where, they noted, her bronze sculptures represent "mythological figures of the Amazon region—vigorous, fantastic, primitive imagery of Senhora Martins's great country."

In the comfort of his own studio, Duchamp would also have had the time to look over the *Amazonia* publication more thoroughly. There is an introduction by Jorge Zarur, who, working for the National Geography Council of Brazil, predictably (citing his position) explains how the Amazon River Basin came into being, and how its geography resulted in the development of diverse but related indigenous tribes. But the text that follows was written by Maria herself and describes the legends that arose from its native inhabitants, each of which is illustrated with a black-and-white photograph of the eight sculptures she created in an effort to bring the Amazonian goddesses to life. A few of these passages might have caught Duchamp's attention, for the majority of the goddesses were portrayed as the ultimate temptresses of men. The river goddess Boìuna, for example, was famous for her ability to consume men:

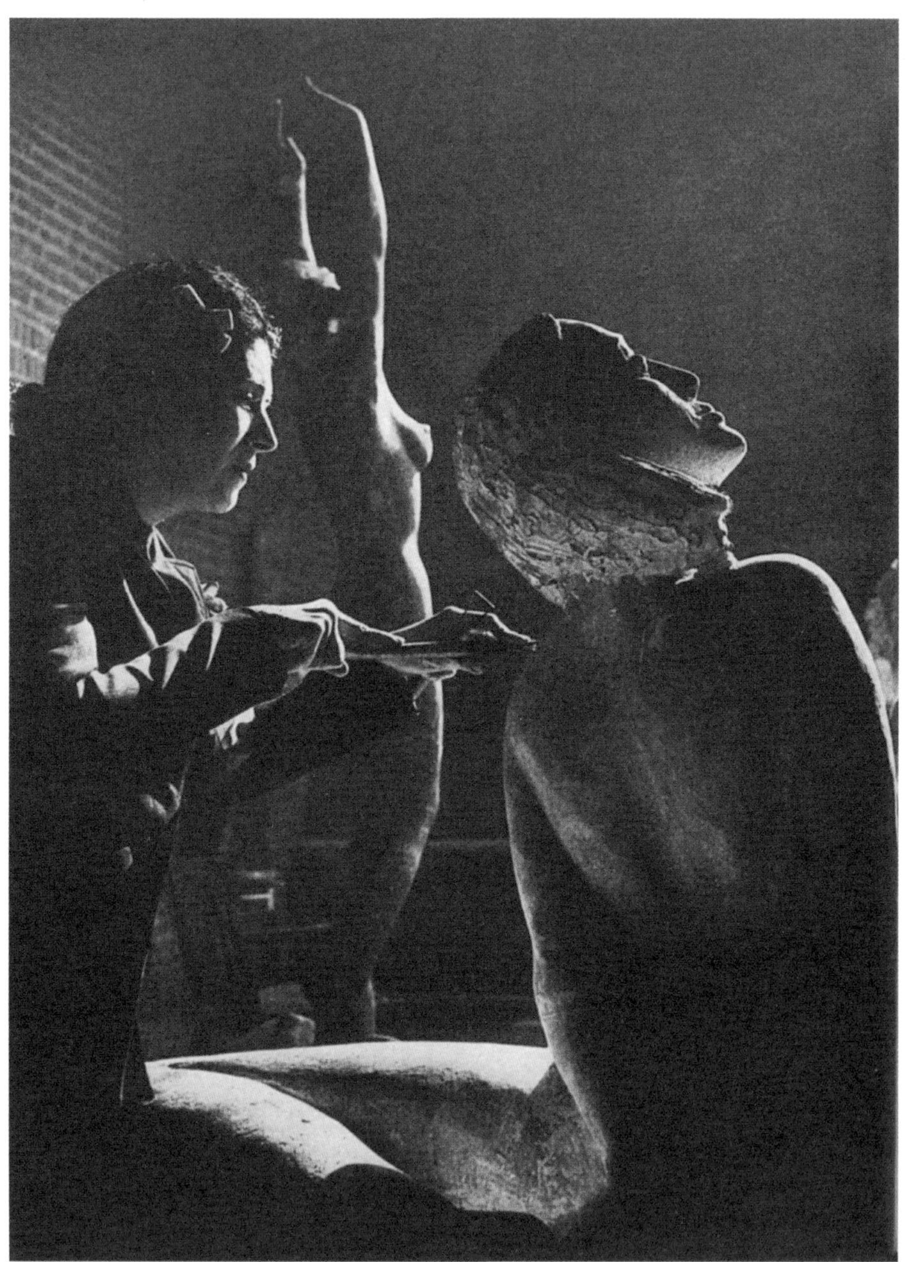

Fig. 4. Maria Martins carving a figure in her
Washington, DC, studio. *Vogue*, April 1, 1943.

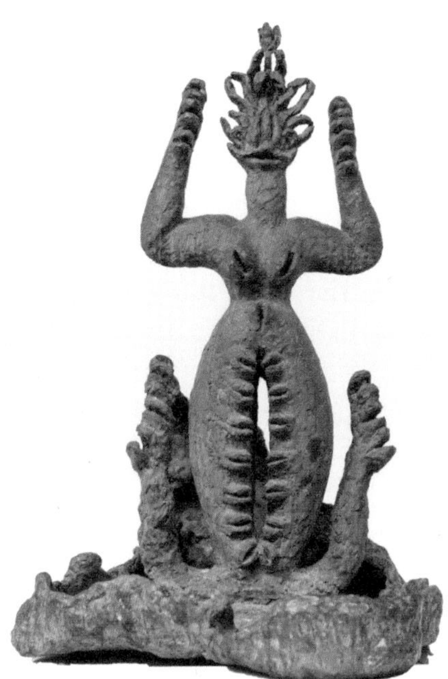

Fig. 5. Maria Martins, *Boìuna*, 1942. Bronze, 28½ × 27 × 18½ in. (72.4 × 68.6 × 47 cm). OAS Art Museum of the Americas, Washington, DC; gift of Nelson Rockefeller.

"sucking their blood, draining their strength." In the sculpture (Fig. 5), the space between her legs opens in the form of a *vagina dentata*, a feature clearly designed to facilitate her male-killing spree. There was also Yara, the enchantress who lives in the Amazon rainforest and seduces men with her song, dragging them down to the depths of the river "until a new love appears," whereupon she "returns to destroy another mortal who cannot resist the temptation of the assassin."

When Duchamp later visited Maria at her studio, he might have learned that a different and much larger version of *Yara* (Fig. 6)—a sculpture over six feet in height and in bronze—had been purchased a year earlier by the

Philadelphia Museum of Art for the impressive sum of $10,000, with funds provided by an anonymous donor, likely Nelson Rockefeller. Although the sculpture was no longer available for view in her studio, Maria might very well have shown Duchamp a photograph of it that she preserved in a scrapbook, showing a nude female figure festooned with remnants of foliage from the river bottom, rising up with her hands clasped between her breasts, exhibiting not a trace of modesty for her lack of clothing. This sculpture would figure prominently in Duchamp's future, but he did not know it at the time. Rockefeller was then Coordinator of Inter-American Affairs for the United States government and used his great wealth to support many artists from Mexico and countries in Central and South America. Two years earlier, he had attended Maria's first retrospective show at the Corcoran Gallery of Art in Washington, DC, and had purchased her more than seven foot tall figure of Christ carved from jacaranda (a deep-rose-colored Brazilian hardwood), which he donated to the Museum of Modern Art in New York. From her *Amazonia* show at the Valentine Gallery, he would purchase six sculptures and donate them to various museums around the United States, including *Boìuna* (Fig. 5), which he gave to the OAS (Organization of American States) Art Museum in Washington, DC.

How much of this information was disclosed to Duchamp at the time is unknown, but he did soon learn that Maria was of sufficient financial means to help support his friend who shared the exhibition. It was likely at Duchamp's suggestion that, with earnings from the sale of her work in the Valentine Gallery show, Maria purchased Mondrian's *Broadway Boogie Woogie*,

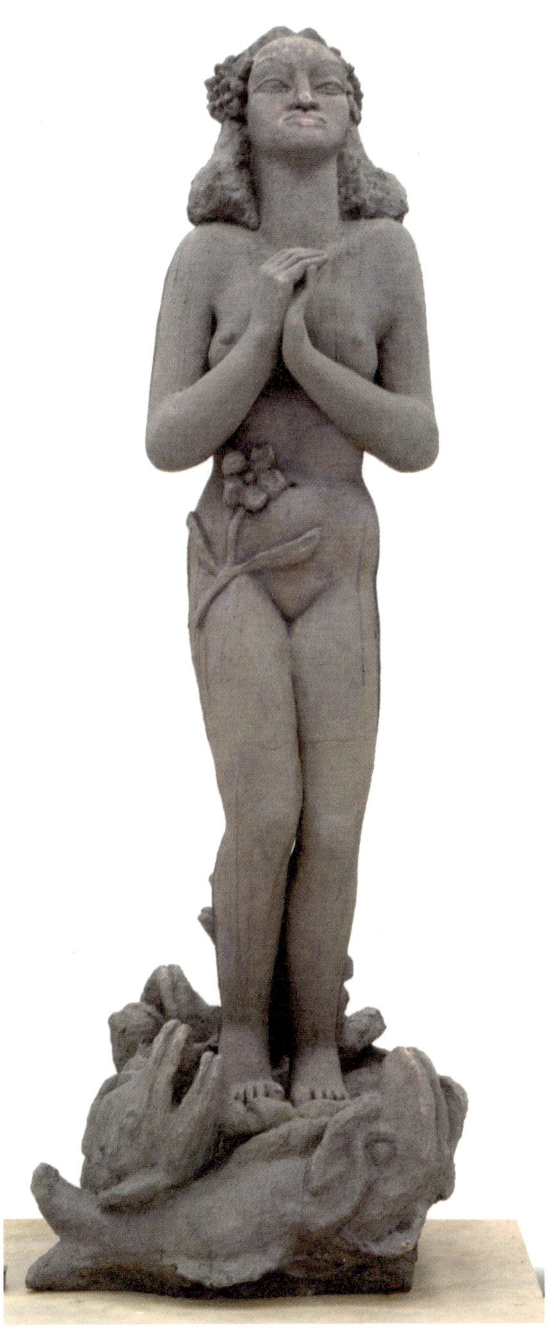

Fig. 6. Maria Martins, *Yara*, 1940. Bronze cast, 1942. Philadelphia Museum of Art; purchased with funds contributed by an anonymous donor, 1942, 1942-72-1.

which was priced at $800, and gave it to the Museum of Modern Art. Of the six paintings by the artist shown in the exhibition, it was the most visually dynamic, for it departed from his usual presentation of large color blocks within black vertical and horizontal black lines, and instead rendered the lines themselves in vibrant colors, echoing the bright lights of Broadway and simulating an overhead view of the rectangular, intersecting streets of New York City. For reasons that are today unknown, at first the museum refused to accept the work, so Maria called Nelson Rockefeller and asked him to intercede. He had earlier served for a brief period as president of the museum. His wealth and expertise carried a great deal of weight, so the work was immediately accepted, and according to family lore, Maria and Duchamp carried the painting themselves over to the museum and presented it to Alfred Barr, the founding director, who received it with open arms and great appreciation.

One of the visitors to Maria's exhibition at the Valentine Gallery was the French Purist painter and theoretician Amédée Ozenfant, who had moved from London to New York in 1939. Later he would take pride in being the "the first to express great enthusiasm" over this exhibition. "I even pronounced the word genius," he later confessed. Among other notable visitors to the show was André Breton, the great French impresario of Surrealism and colleague of Duchamp, who was living out the war years in New York. Breton must have gotten along rather well with Maria, for she spoke French fluently, and Breton refused to speak English. He immediately proclaimed his admiration for the Amazonia group. "Maria has succeeded marvelously in capturing at their

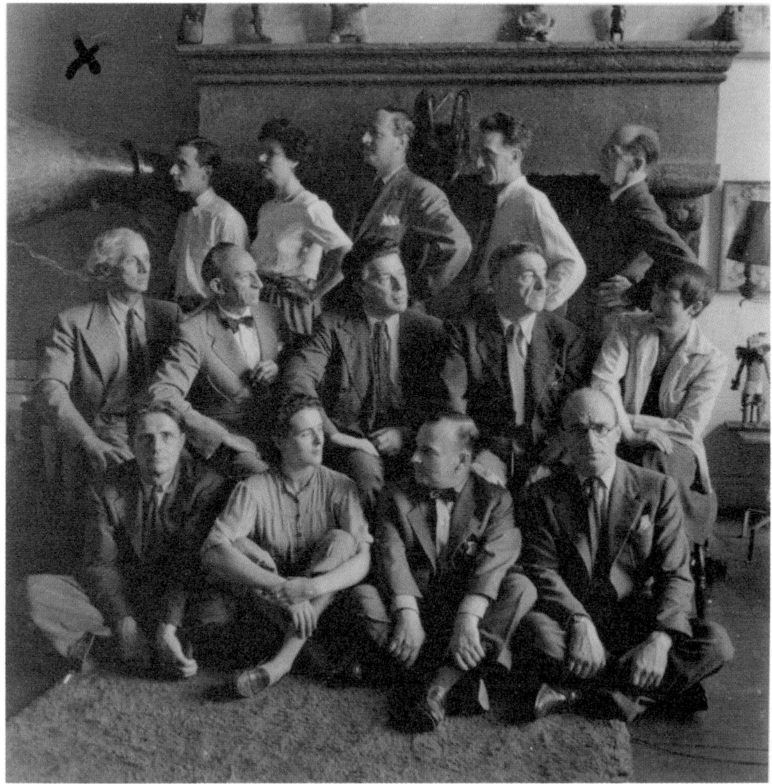

Fig. 7. *Europeans in Exile*, 1942. Front row, from left to right: Stanley William Hayter, Leonora Carrington, Frederick Kiesler, Kurt Seligmann; second row: Max Ernst, Amédée Ozenfant, André Breton, Fernand Léger, Berenice Abbott; third row: Jimmy Ernst, Peggy Guggenheim, John Ferren, Marcel Duchamp, Piet Mondrian. Photograph by Hermann Landshoff. Marcel Duchamp Exhibition Records, Philadelphia Museum of Art, Library and Archives.

primitive source not only anguish, temptation and fever," he wrote a few years later, "but also the surprise, happiness and calm, and even occasionally pure delight." It was likely through both Breton and Duchamp that Maria was introduced to the circle of Surrealists

who were also living in New York during the war—
André Masson, Stanley William Hayter, Yves Tanguy,
Kay Sage, Max Ernst, Matta Echaurren, Kurt Seligmann, Leonora Carrington, and Marcel Duchamp—
all of whom and others were memorably captured in
a photograph taken a year earlier in the apartment of
Peggy Guggenheim (Fig. 7), the wealthy heiress and art
collector, who had moved to New York herself just a
year earlier. As Maria's relationship with these artists
intensified, the influence of Surrealism became increasingly apparent in her work, so much so that by the late
1940s Maria Martins could be accurately described as
one of the most important and accomplished Surrealist
sculptors of her generation.

Breton believed that myth was an essential component of life, a common factor that united the peoples
of all places at all times, which is why he maintained a
lifelong fascination for all forms of so-called primitive
(non-Western) art. As a result, he was probably immediately attracted to Maria's exploration of a legend drawn
from deep within the Amazon jungle. Her twisting,
entangled forms—many of which seem to emerge from
entwined branches and underwater vegetation—might
have been seen by Breton as the three-dimensional
equivalent of psychic automatism, which he defined
as the expression of thought without the imposition of
reason and/or aesthetic concerns. Works that reflected
this modus operandi were shown in Maria's next show
at the Valentine Gallery, which was held in the spring
of 1944. A photograph of the artist taken next to one
of the works included in this exhibition—*Ma Chanson*
(My Song)—shows her bearing a marked degree of
confidence, equal to the power displayed in the bronze

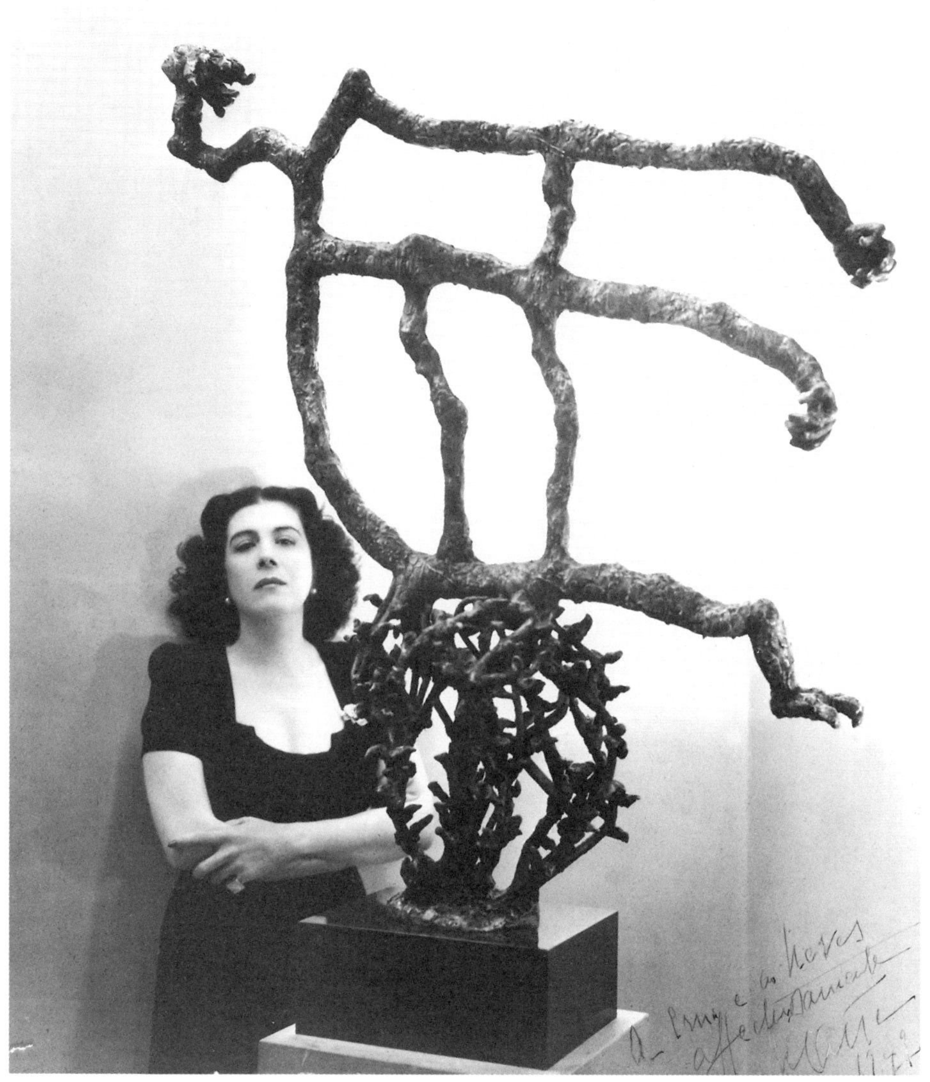

Fig. 8. Maria standing next to her sculpture *Ma Chanson* (My Song),
1944. Photograph c. 1946.

sculpture she created, an essentially abstract entanglement of branches that end in claw-like protrusions (Fig. 8). In addition to the sculpture, eight examples of gold "sculptured jewelry" were also included in the show. A statement in the catalogue noted that all of the works were made by means of the "old 'lost wax' (*cire perdue*) technique," explaining that since the original wax sculpture and its plaster mold are destroyed through the casting process, each object was unique. One reviewer traced the stylistic sources of Maria's work to "the rococo, the ornate sculpture of India, and something akin to the work of Jacques Lipchitz." The similarity to work by this Lithuanian-born sculptor is not coincidental, as Maria had studied bronze-casting techniques with him for several years after she took her apartment in New York. The same critic who noticed the similarity in their work singled out one of the sculptures for the trouble it must have given those who had to cast it into bronze, but he felt that most of the works "strain at form rather than significance." Taking a similar position, Clement Greenberg, who reviewed the show for his weekly column in *The Nation*, proclaimed the work to be "the last living manifestation of academic sculpture." Apparently, it did not fit in with his belief that all works of art were required to reflect the nature of the material from which they were made. "The metal almost denies itself in this monstrous and happy proliferation of plant and animal forms," he wrote. He found the design "symmetrical," the formal relations "transparent and predictable." Nevertheless, he concluded that Maria had "immense talent," singling out several sculptures and jewelry, "which," he said, "are the best contemporary examples I have seen."

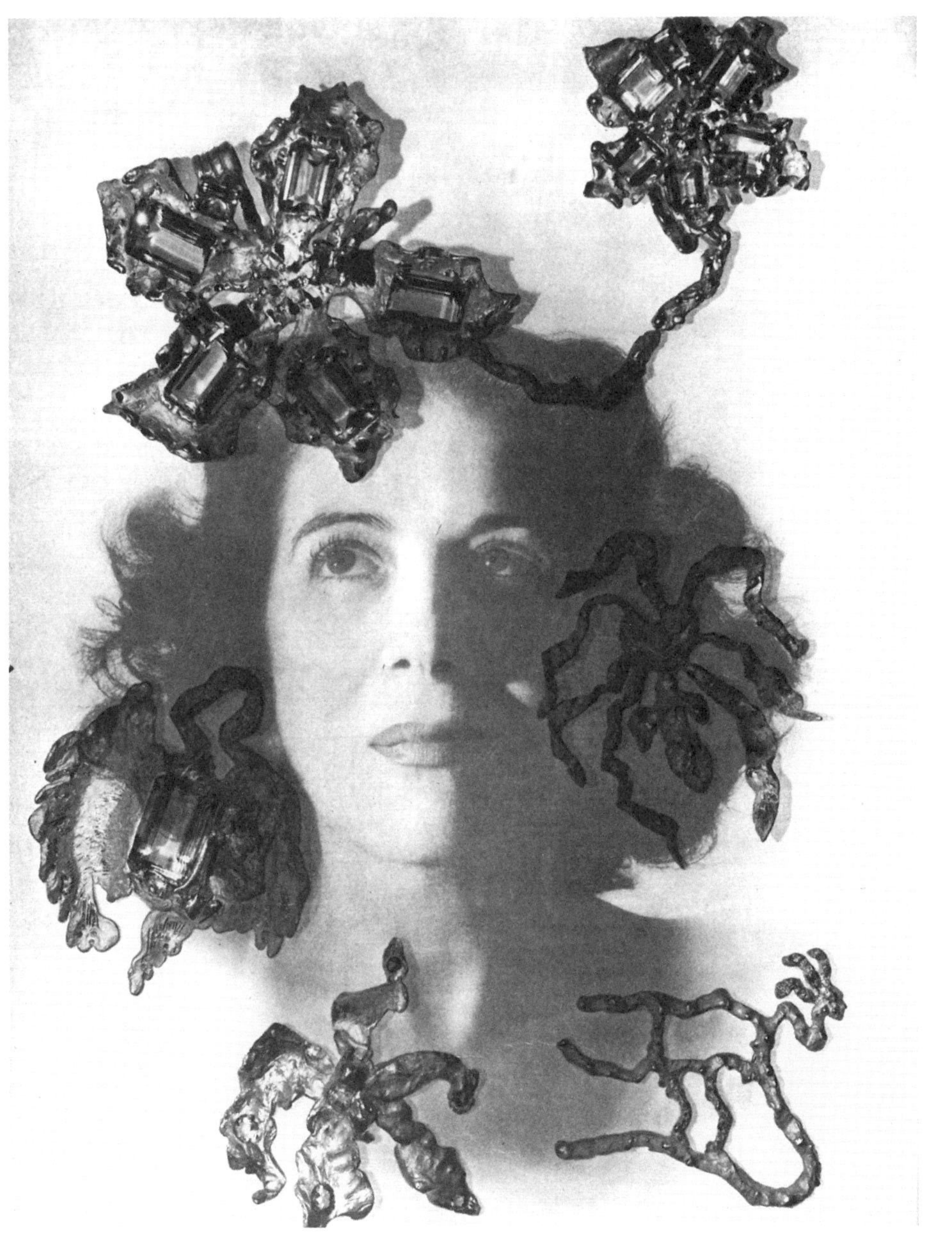

Fig. 9. Maria Martins's portrait surrounded by examples of her jewelry.
Vogue, July 1, 1944.

A month after this review appeared, *Vogue* magazine ran a second notice on Maria, including her in a group of rising female stars (Fig. 9). Considering the nature of the magazine, it is not surprising that they were more interested in her jewelry than in her sculpture, and the notice featured a portrait photograph of the artist seen behind a plate of glass onto which were mounted six examples of her jewelry, one of which (reproduced in the lower-right corner) clearly derived from the form of her sculpture (Fig. 8). "Her jewels coin emotion in metal," an accompanying text explained, "the sorcerer's snarls of dull gold, gilt-edged, dusted with diamonds, chunked with semi-precious stone." The designer of the layout is uncredited, although it is tempting to suspect that Duchamp might have had something to do with it, for he was by then already well known for his masterpiece on glass, *The Bride Stripped Bare by Her Bachelors, Even*, 1915–23, which was owned by the collector Katherine Dreier, but which had then been on view at the Museum of Modern Art as part of a temporary exhibition (Fig. 18).

FALLING

By the fall of 1943, Duchamp began making increasingly frequent visits to Maria's home and studio at 471 Park Avenue, on the corner of 58th Street and around the corner from the Valentine Gallery. She rented a fairly lavish three-bedroom duplex apartment, with a large lower room that she used as her studio (Fig. 10). During several of his visits, Duchamp met Maria's teenage daughter, Nora, who visited her mother in New York when she was on leave from a boarding school she attended in Virginia. Nora recalled that Duchamp was a continuous presence at the apartment, a situation she did not find in the least bit uncomfortable, for apparently her father accepted it as well, since he adored his wife and was willing to tolerate any deviations from their marriage that made her happy. The studio was a large, double-height room with floor-to-ceiling windows, in which she worked and displayed her sculpture. A painting by Léger dominated one wall and dark, serpentine sculptures with outstretched arms and protruding fingers inhabited the rest of the space. Maria also likely visited Duchamp. Ever since he returned to the United States in 1942, he had been living in the homes

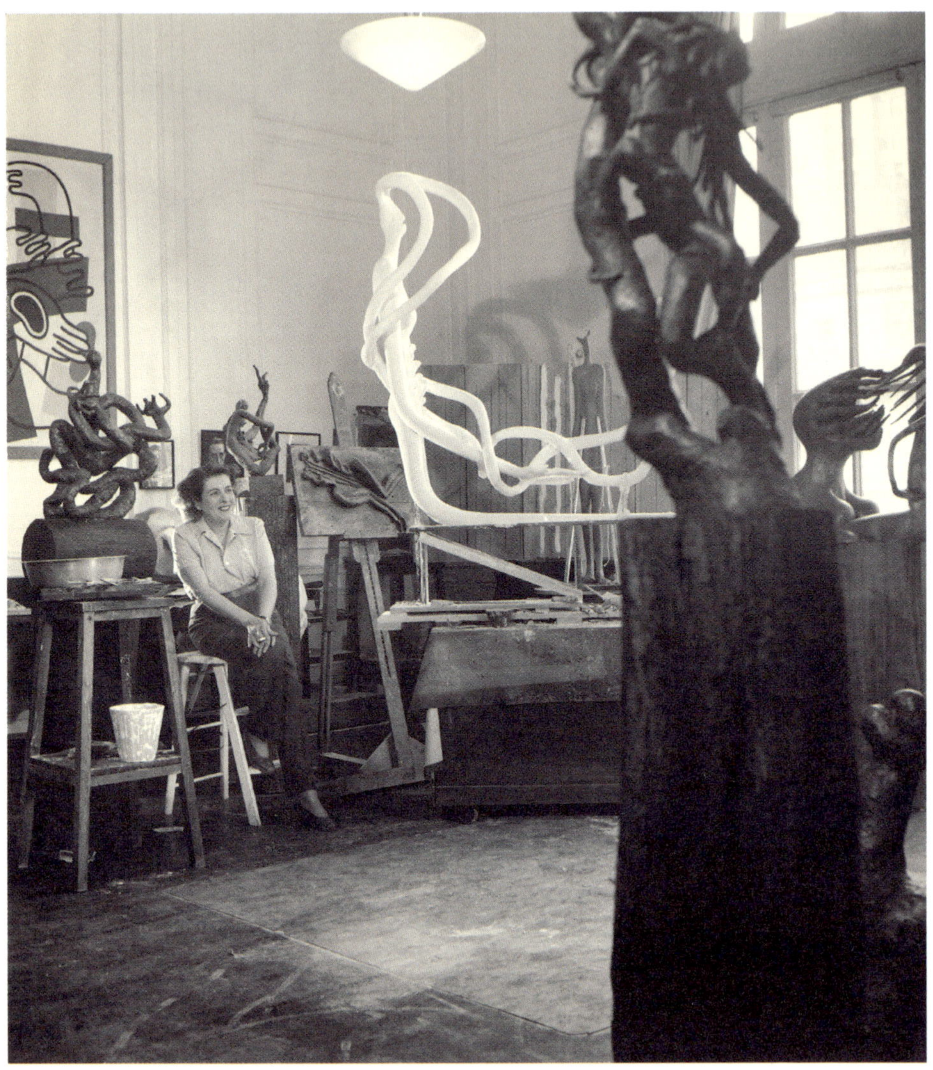

Fig. 10. Maria Martins in her Park Avenue studio, c. 1946. Photographer unknown. Collection Ignez Ceglia Simoes, Coconut Grove, Florida.

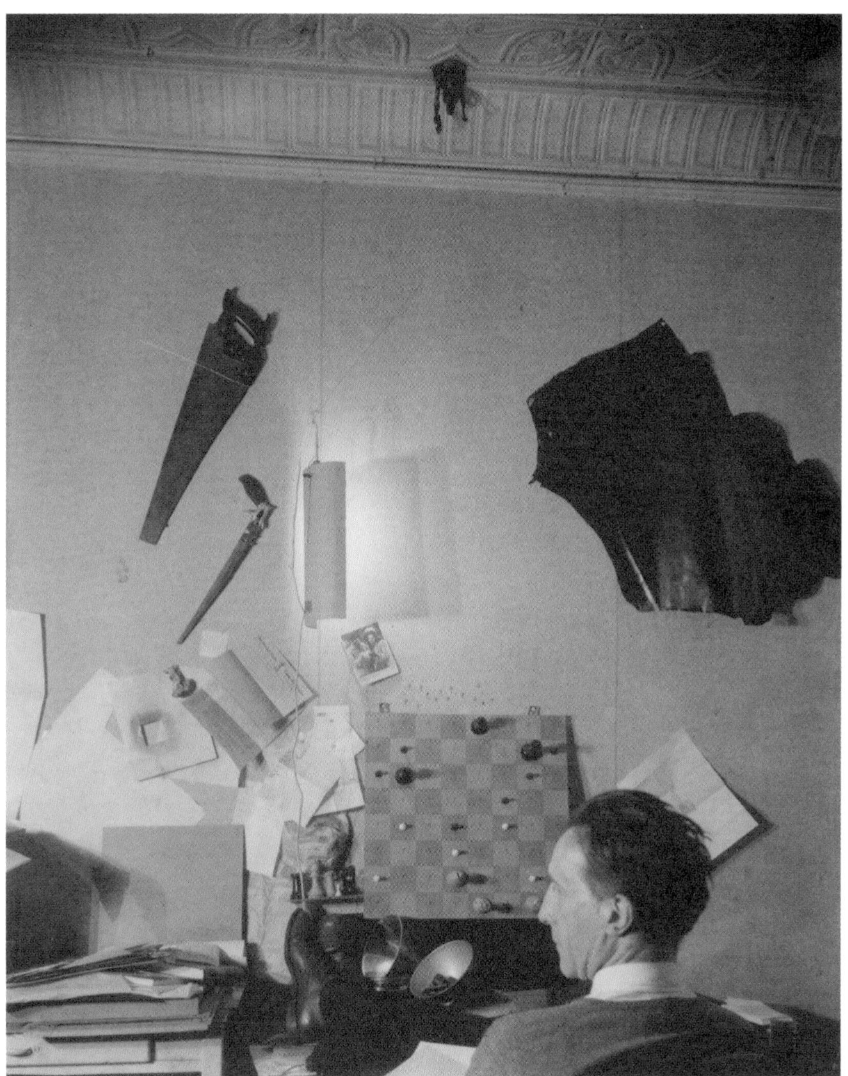

Fig. 11. Marcel Duchamp at the desk in his 14th Street studio, 1945.
Photograph by Percy Rainford for Frederick Kiesler's triptych in *View* magazine.

of friends, but in October 1943, he rented a small studio apartment for $35 per month in a five-floor walkup on 14th Street near Seventh Avenue. He shared a bathroom with two neighbors and kept the space sparsely furnished: a table, desk, and chair; a variety of objects hanging on the wall; and a chessboard always in view where he could study certain game positions at leisure (Fig. 11). There were none of the accoutrements usually associated with the studio of an active painter or sculptor. Certainly there was no smell of paints and turpentine, which he abhorred, seeking as always to separate himself from anything that could identify him as a traditional artist. He still needed a space in which to work on whatever projects he became involved with, and now he also needed a place that could offer yet another refuge to rendezvous with Maria, a place far from Midtown and from the watchful eyes of others. Their increasingly frequent meetings could be looked upon critically by even well-intentioned friends, and Maria would not want to jeopardize her public image as the faithful and loving wife of the Brazilian ambassador to the United States.

Exactly what the two artists talked about when they met is difficult to reconstruct. The subject of politics must have come up, for after all the war was then raging in Europe, but they both believed it was not an artist's responsibility to express their political beliefs through their work. Certainly they both agreed that freedom and preventing oppression of any type were values worth fighting for, but, at the core, they were confirmed pacifists. When Duchamp moved to America after the outbreak of World War I, he told a journalist that he admired "the attitude of combating invasion with folded arms." Even though Maria was married to a diplomat whose job was to interact with the politicians of his day, he complained that his wife found it all tedious, and the only thing that interested her was her involvement in the world of art, a complaint with which she had trouble disagreeing. Did the two artists exchange ideas about their work? Maria might have told him about hers, about the artists she studied with and the various techniques she employed, but unless it was within the context of a formal interview, Duchamp was reticent to speak about his. We know that when he moved to New York during the years of the First World War, whenever a visitor to his apartment asked about the ready-mades—a bicycle wheel mounted on a stool stood in the middle of the apartment, a snow shovel hung from the ceiling—he usually said only, *Cela n'a pas d'importance*. Essentially, he dismissed their significance and, therefore, avoided a philosophical discussion of their aesthetic merit, a serious and complicated conversation that would have seemed inappropriate within the context of a casual friendship.

If anything, Duchamp might have told Maria about his *Boîte-en-valise*, a small suitcase into which he had packed miniature reproductions of his most important work, which he planned for an edition of 300 copies. He labored on this project for some five years before coming to New York, gathering reproductions, arranging for them to be colored by means of pochoir, and assembling the contents into a cardboard box that neatly folded into a leather attaché case. He sold the first example in 1941 to Peggy Guggenheim (Fig. 12), who was then living in Grenoble (having escaped the Occupied Zone in Paris), and who had volunteered to ship some contents

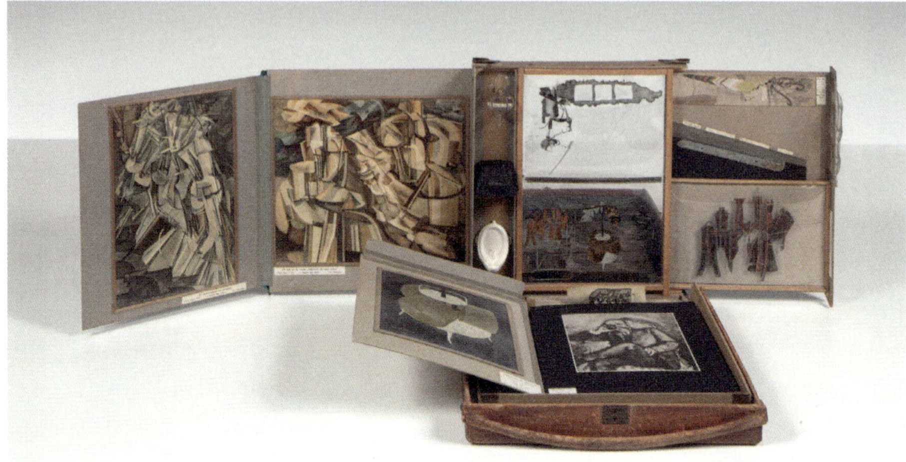

Fig. 12. Marcel Duchamp, *de ou par MARCEL DUCHAMP ou RROSE
SELAVY* (from or by MARCEL DUCHAMP or RROSE SELAVY),
or *La Boîte-en-valise* (The Box in a Valise), 1936 (Series A), deluxe edition,
1941. Peggy Guggenheim Foundation, Venice.

of the valise to New York with her household goods.
When she left for America a few months later, she took
the valise with her and displayed it for the first time in
her gallery, The Art of This Century, which opened on
West 57th Street in New York in October 1942. It is not
known if Maria saw this show, but there is no reason
to imagine she had not. She had recently moved into
her New York apartment and, like many other artists,
made it a practice to visit most of the galleries in the
city that showed contemporary art, particularly those
on 57th Street, right around the corner from her studio. If she had seen the Guggenheim show, she would
have had a hard time forgetting Duchamp's valise, as
it was displayed in an elaborate structure designed by
Frederick Kiesler. Visitors were instructed to turn a large

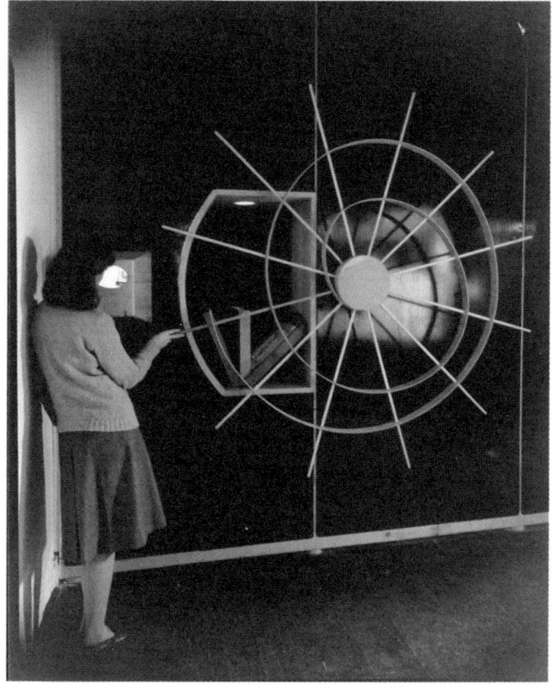

Fig. 13. Frederick Kiesler's viewing device used
to see elements from Marcel Duchamp's
Boîte-en-valise, Art of This Century Gallery, October
1942. Photograph by Berenice Abbott. Fralin
Museum of Art, University of Virginia; gift of
Mr. and Mrs. Harry Bum.

spiral-shaped wheel and look through a peephole in
the wall (Fig. 13), whereupon fourteen images from the
work would rotate separately into view. (The complete
suitcase was shown in an adjacent showcase.) If Maria
had not seen this show, she still would have known
about the valise, as countless reproductions for it filled
the space where Duchamp lived, and she would likely
have seen the photograph of him that appeared in the

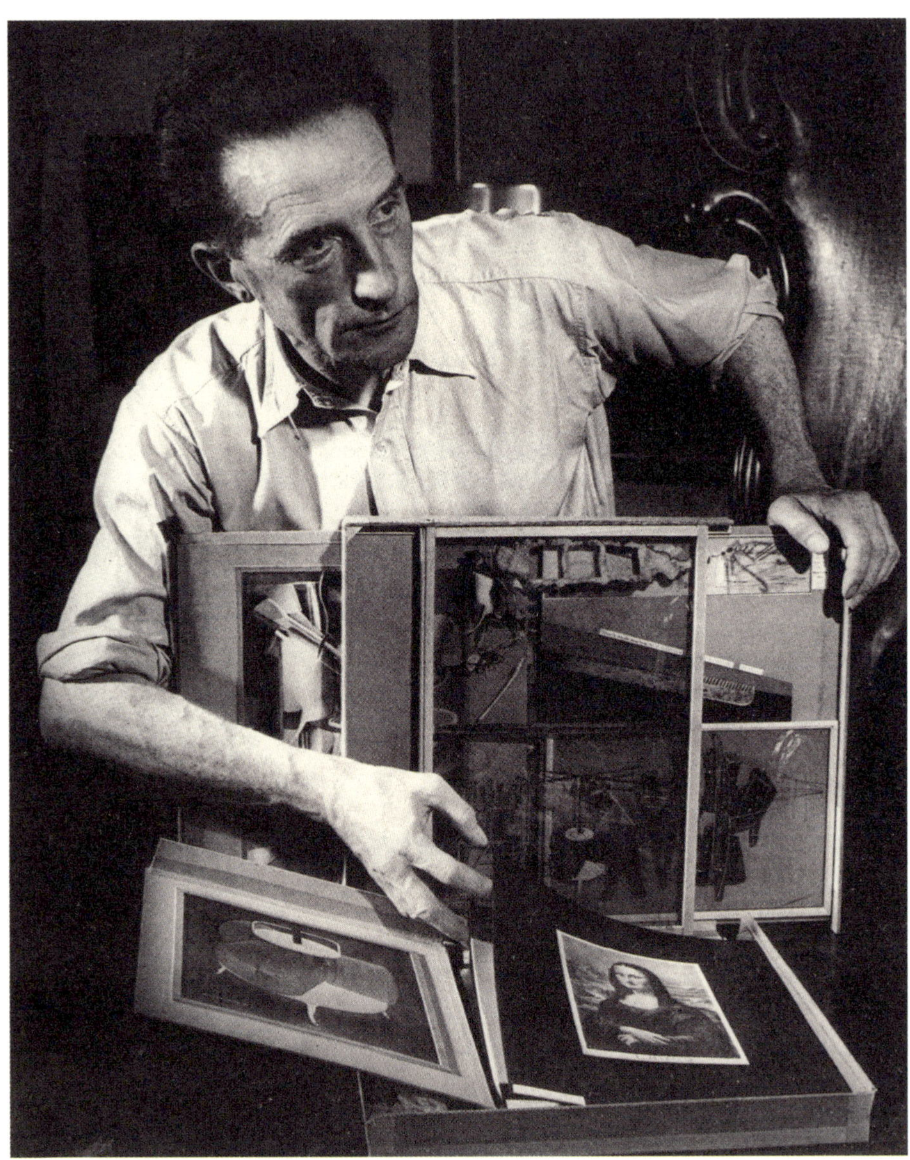

Fig. 14. Marcel Duchamp displaying his *Boîte-en-valise* in the townhouse of Peggy Guggenheim, New York, August 1942 (reproduced in *Time* magazine, September 1942).

September issue of *Time* magazine, which shows him in Peggy Guggenheim's apartment displaying its contents (Fig. 14). If they talked about why he was recycling his past, he could very well have told her about his disdain for artists who repeated themselves just for the purpose of attaining fame and fortune. With this project he was essentially creating a three-dimensional album of his earlier work, not making something that was a mere stylistic derivation of what he had become known for with the intent of advancing his career. Instead, he was confronting the issue of replication directly—using the very process to refute its profit-driven motives—just as Parisians tell you that the only way to avoid seeing the Eiffel Tower is to climb up into its structure and view the city from there.

Certainly both Marcel and Maria believed that artists were required to make unique contributions to the art of their times, challenging those who came before them. When Duchamp was asked some ten years earlier if he had any advice for young artists, he responded in Oedipal terms: "The son must hate the father in order to be a good son," adding "such hatred seems to be the only means of producing that necessary reaction against the achievements of the previous period." She would have likely agreed with this opinion, although she would have expressed it differently. "There is no alternative in art," she later explained. "Be a pioneer, be a creator, or stay quiet." To which she added: "Creation is a solitary act and even though painters and sculptors abound here and there, eternal art is reserved for the few capable of great sacrifices and great flights to almost unattainable heights, surrendering without reservation to their gods or their inner demons." At this point, Duchamp might have brought up his well-known disdain for the commercialization of art, treading rather lightly on the topic, since Maria's work was selling so well at the Valentine Gallery. It is possible that they might have discussed philosophies of life, he finding emotional commitment a restriction to his personal freedom, whereas she argued that freedom could be in itself restrictive. "This is the great danger of liberation," she would say, because "one becomes a slave to freedom."

Whatever they talked about, there can be no question that Duchamp found himself increasingly drawn—both physically and emotionally—to this alluring and engaging woman from the tropics, yet he realized that because she was married with three teenage children, she could hardly extricate herself from her domestic life and become a permanent fixture in his. He expressed his frustration in a unique endgame problem he had devised in chess, which he had printed on an announcement for an exhibition at the Julien Levy Gallery in New York held in December of 1943, just over nine months after he met Maria (Fig. 15). The show was called "Through the Big End of the Opera Glass" (inspired by Lewis Carroll's *Through the Looking Glass*) and, as the title implies, featured exceptionally small work. Years later, Levy explained that the idea had come from viewing an example of Duchamp's *Boîte-en-valise*.

At first glance, the chessboard on the announcement is not visible. What can be seen is only the figure of a Cupid shooting an arrow downward toward the ground, which Duchamp drew and signed. The endgame is visible only when you hold the Cupid up against light, whereupon a chessboard immediately comes into

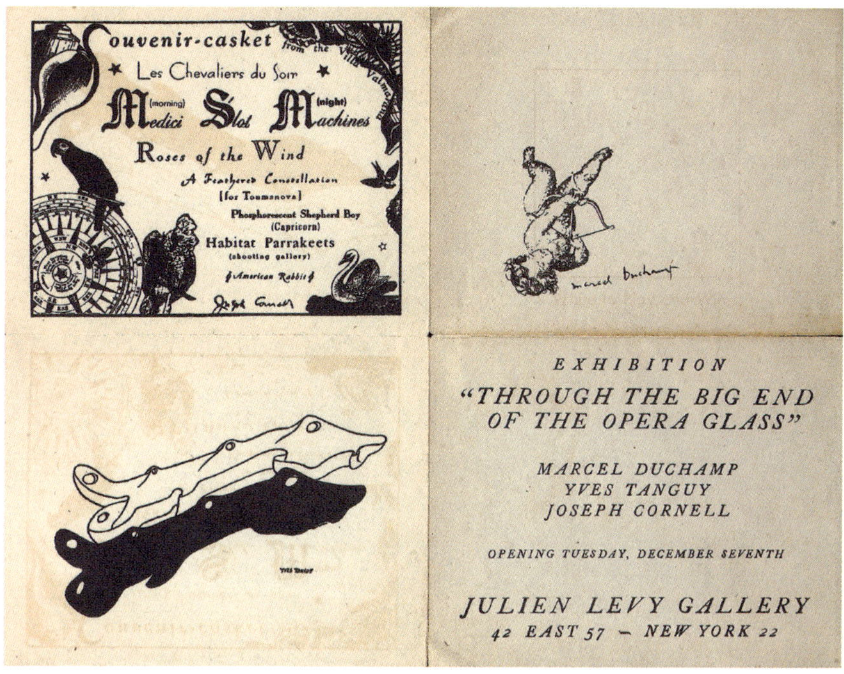
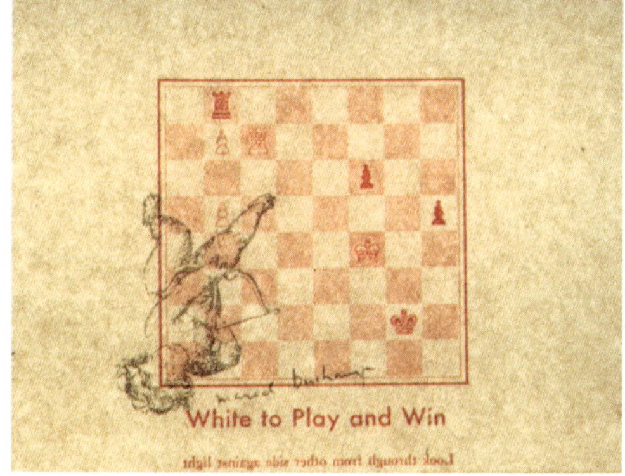

Fig. 15. Marcel Duchamp, *Cupid*, 1943. Announcement for the exhibition *Through the Big End of the Opera Glass*, Julien Levy Gallery, New York, December 7–28, 1943. Detail: chess diagram seen through *Cupid*. Collection Francis M. Naumann and Marie T. Keller, Yorktown Heights, New York.

view with the words printed below: "White to Play and Win." According to these instructions, chess players are to move a white piece first and force a win. As chess analysts and computer engines would later prove, however, with this particular endgame problem, white can never win, no matter how precisely play continues. Even if you follow the "hint" provided by the cupid's arrow and advance a pawn forward, white still cannot win. If a win is not possible, why then set up this situation in the first place? Duchamp became known for something he said whenever anyone experienced difficulty in understanding works of art. "There is no solution," he would say, "because there is no problem." In other words, do not assume the work of art is presenting a problem, and you can enjoy it for exactly what it is, without thinking that you have to solve its inner secrets to fully understand its meaning. Moreover, in his design for the announcement, Duchamp alludes to its underlying meaning by using a Cupid to suggest the first move for white. Cupid is a well-known symbol of romance, not the sort of figure associated with the game of chess, but rather the mythological child or boy god of erotic love and desire, the prick of his arrow causing his victim to fall helplessly in love. No matter what white does, nothing can result in its victory. In Duchamp's case, his attempt to secure the affections of Maria are just like his endgame position: a problem with no solution.

Julien Levy was among the few of Duchamp's friends who would have understood the rationale behind this endgame problem. He not only knew about Duchamp's relationship with Maria, but he played chess with the artist on a regular basis. A month after the exhibition closed, Duchamp gave Levy yet another gift that only he could understand, a deluxe valise containing within its lid the maquette he had used a few months earlier for a special edition of *VVV* magazine. It featured the torso of a nude female figure cut out of paper and placed against a segment of chicken wire, but here the woman's body is inscribed with the words *La forchette du cavalier* (Knight's Fork), writing that begins from the figure's nipples and ends at her crotch (Fig. 16). In chess, a knight's fork refers to the knight attacking at least two pieces simultaneously, so that no matter how the opponent responds, he is likely to lose one of them. Anyone who has experienced a fork of this type—particularly one in which the knight attacks two more powerful pieces—knows how frustrating the experience can be, for in most cases there is little that can be done except to try salvaging the more powerful piece. It is especially painful when your opponent checks your king and attacks your queen in the same move, what is called the Royal Fork, as you are obligated to move your king and, therefore, lose your queen. In Duchamp's construction, the simplified shape of the torso mimes the shape of a chess piece, an allusion the artist may well have intended. For all we know, Duchamp might very well have confided in Levy that he and Maria found themselves trapped in a cage (a reference to the chicken wire used to entrap this figure), the very word he would use to describe their situation in letters he wrote to her a few years later.

As they saw more and more of each other, it seems reasonable to imagine that Marcel and Maria visited the Museum of Modern Art together in its new Bauhaus-style building on 53rd Street between Fifth

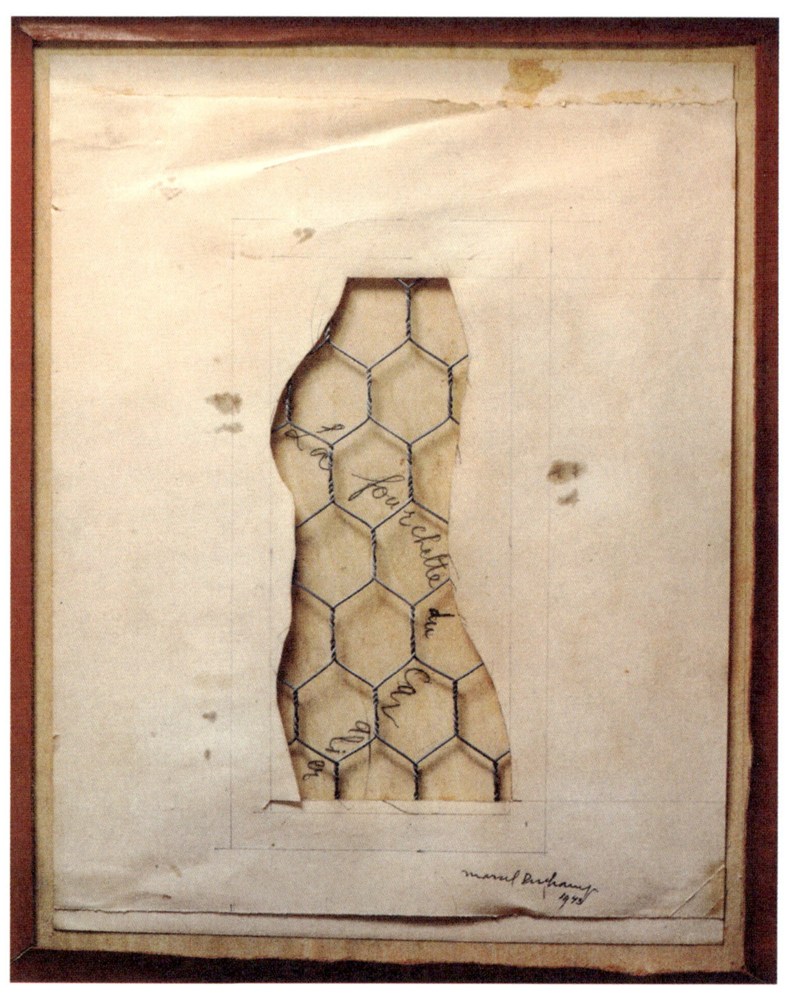

Fig 16. Marcel Duchamp, *La forchette du cavalier* (The Knight's Fork), 1943. Construction with paper and chicken wire mounted into the lid of a deluxe *Boîte-en-valise*. Bluff Collection.

and Sixth Avenues (the same location it occupies to this day). They certainly would have had a reason to view the Mondrian exhibition held there in the spring of 1945, a sort of memorial to the artist who had died the previous year. There his *Broadway Boogie Woogie*—which they were both instrumental in bringing to the museum—was placed on prominent display, hanging alongside other works by the artist made or reworked during his last years in New York (Fig. 17). While they were at the museum, it is difficult to imagine that Duchamp would not have taken Martins upstairs to show her his *Large Glass*, the monumental work of art he had constructed during his first American sojourn, but which he left in a state of intentional incompletion in 1923. The work was borrowed in 1943 from the collection of Katherine S. Dreier for an exhibition called "Art in Progress," but it remained at the museum on temporary, extended loan (Fig. 18). It was positioned next to two paintings by Pablo Picasso and opposite Roger de La Fresnaye's *The Conquest of Air*, a large Cubist picture from 1913. *The Large Glass* was installed at a ninety degree angle to the wall, so that its internal components cast prominent shadows on the wall behind it.

As they looked up together at the construction (Fig. 19), Duchamp might have explained to Maria how the elements within its design were meant to "function," that is to say, how the Bride occupying the upper register of the composition attracted the interest of nine Bachelors in the lower register. He called it *The Bride Stripped Bare by Her Bachelors, Even.* In essence, it was the portrayal of an elaborate lovemaking machine, one whose construction he had abandoned some twenty years earlier when he decided the tedium of physically

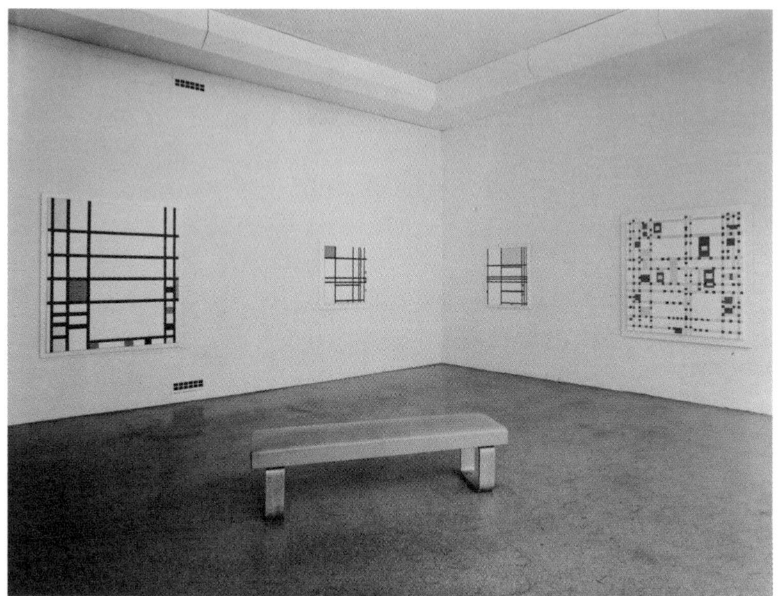

Fig. 17. *Piet Mondrian*, March 21–May 13, 1945, Museum of Modern Art, New York. Installation view showing *Broadway Boogie Woogie* at right. Photograph by Soichi Sunami.

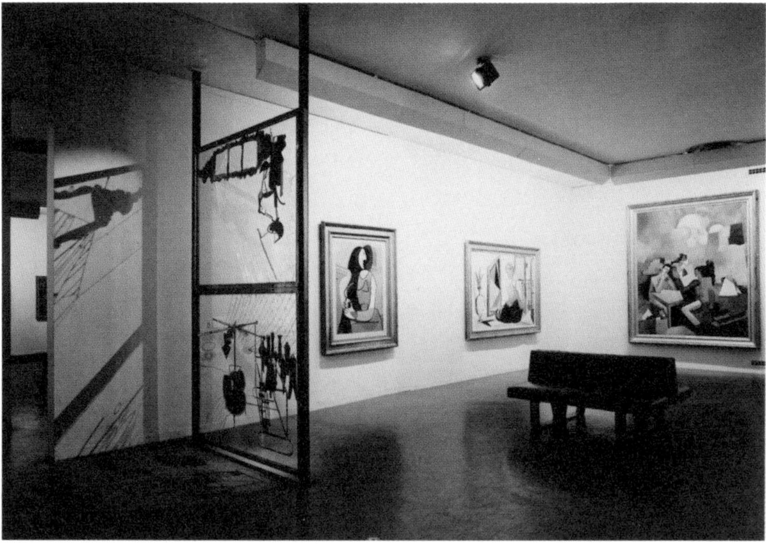

Fig. 18. "Painting, Sculpture, Prints," in the series *Art in Progress: 15th Anniversary Exhibition*, May 24–October 15, 1944, Museum of Modern Art, New York. Installation view, showing Duchamp's *Large Glass* next to two paintings by Picasso and opposite Roger de La Fresnaye's *The Conquest of Air.*

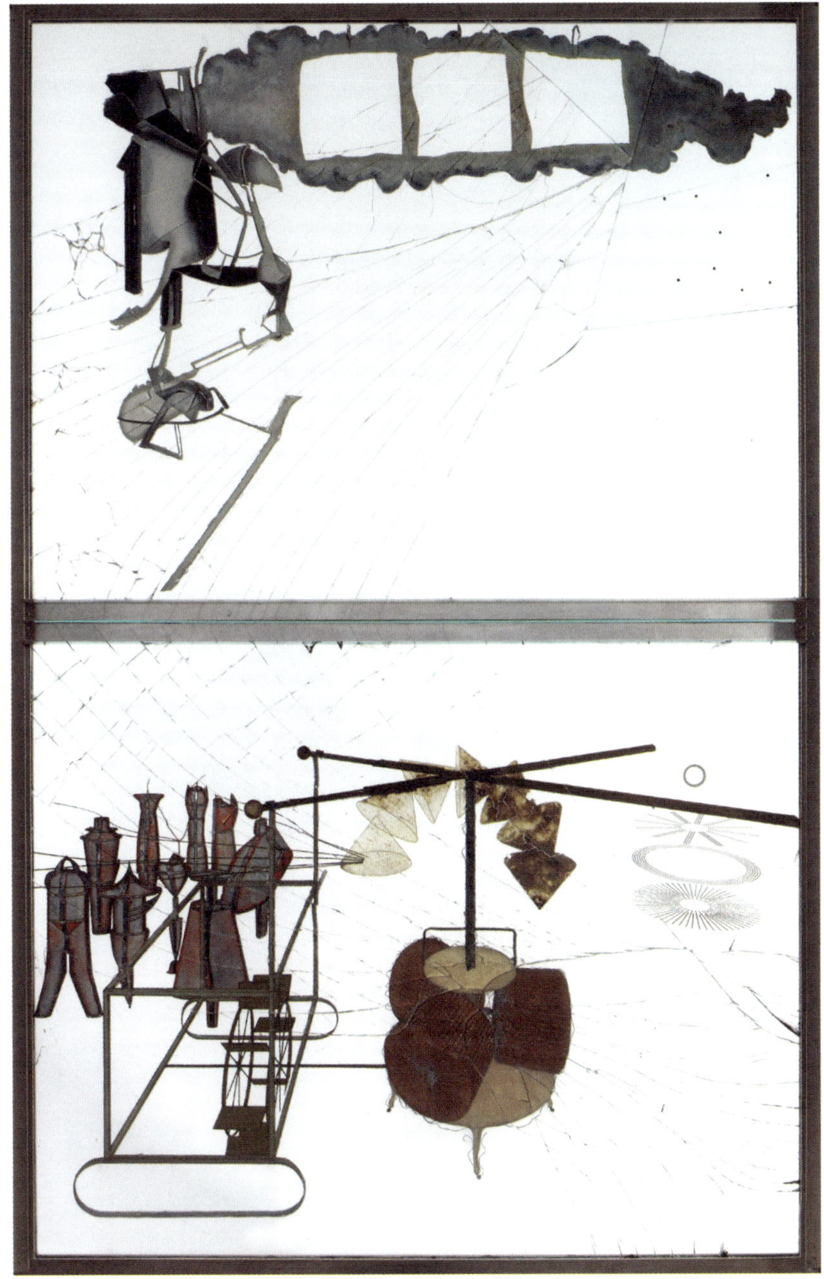

Fig. 19. Marcel Duchamp, *The Bride Stripped Bare by Her Bachelors, Even (The Large Glass)*, 1915–23. Oil, varnish, lead foil, lead wire, and dust on two glass panels, 109¼ × 70 × 3⅜ in. (277 × 178 × 9 cm). Philadelphia Museum of Art; bequest of Katherine S. Dreier, 1952.

finishing it was something with which he had grown tired and bored. In his usual self-effacing manner, he is unlikely to have told Maria that the very fact that this was a painting made on the surface of glass was in itself revolutionary, something no one had ever tried before on this grand scale. The medium had its shortcomings, however, as he likely pointed out, because the glass panels smashed while in transit after an exhibition. He considered this a sort of happy accident, a chance occurrence that had completed the work. He spent a month at Dreier's home in West Redding, Connecticut, painstakingly gluing all the broken shards back into their original position. He especially liked the way the cracks created a radiating pattern, one above that reflected the one below (since the two panels were detached from their support and transported facing one another when the break occurred).

Duchamp did not likely have to explain to Maria that this elaborate construction was somewhat self-referential, as when he made it, he was himself a bachelor in pursuit of a bride, although he never did attain union with her. How much they discussed their prior love lives is difficult to say, although the topic must have come up, as it does inevitably with most people who share—or who are about to share—an intimate relationship. If he talked about his past, he might have told Maria that he was himself once married, but that it was more an experiment than the sanctified union of an emotional bond; although she seemed to have fallen in love with him, her affections were not reciprocated, so the marriage eventually dissolved. Maria might have told Marcel that she, too, had been married before her present husband, to a well-known Brazilian historian with whom she had two daughters, one of whom died of tuberculosis when she was only three years old. Maria was only twenty-one years old at the time of that marriage, and it lasted only a few years. She accompanied her husband to an international conference on immigration in Rome, where she met and began a brief affair with—of all people—Benito Mussolini, the prime minister of Italy, who was just then in the process of transforming his country into a Fascist state. It was at that moment when her current husband, Carlos Martins, who was then Brazilian chargé d'affaires in London, came to Rome and, according to what she later told her daughters, snatched her from the arms of the Italian dictator. They married in Paris in 1926 and, for the next eighteen years, she accompanied her husband in his various diplomatic posts, to Ecuador, France, Denmark, Japan, Belgium, and finally to Washington, DC, where he was now serving as ambassador to the United States.

Duchamp's social life was—by comparison—fairly uneventful. He spent the better part of the years between the wars playing chess at various tournaments in Europe, and his closest female companion in Paris was an American by the name of Mary Reynolds, who was now temporarily living in an apartment in Greenwich Village to escape the war in Europe. Although he had been with her for some twenty years, they never lived together, and though he cared for her deeply, he had to confess that he was never really in love with her, at least not to the extent that he would consider marriage. He saw her now only infrequently and rarely in a public setting. He might have told Maria that when he was young, he, too, had a child, which no one knew about.

When he was only twenty-three years old, he got one of his models pregnant and she had a daughter, but she brought up that child as hers, so, for all he knew, she did not even know he existed. He saw her once by chance in the Métro holding her mother's hand, but, other than that, he had no contact with her whatsoever. He was, in effect, still a bachelor in search of his bride, but standing in front of his *Large Glass* with Maria, he probably determined that—at long last—he had found the woman of his dreams. In their shared exchange about prior relationships, it is doubtful that Maria would have told Duchamp about her more recent dalliances, such as her brief but tumultuous affair with the sculptor Jacques Lipchitz, with whom she spent some time learning various bronze-casting techniques. He fell madly in love with her, but the feelings were not reciprocated—they rarely were with the men in Maria's life. According to several subsequent scholars, Lipchitz was lucky to have gotten away as cleanly as he did, having experienced "a narrow escape from what he perceived to be the clutches of a ferocious, man-eating goddess whose siren call he was doomed never to forget."

Martins was the classic femme fatale, a seductress who did whatever she needed to get a man to fall in love with her, while never falling in love herself. That way, she could exercise control over the relationship, a position she would protect at any cost. She reportedly became extremely jealous if these men demonstrated the slightest degree of affection for another woman. The more time he spent with Maria, the more Duchamp became seduced by her charms, but the frustration of being unable to win over her affections completely must have been a painful experience. He expressed precisely these sentiments bluntly and poignantly in a gift that he gave her in 1946 called *Paysage fautif* (Faulty Landscape), an image that, at first, appears entirely abstract, something possibly created with a light wash of viscous pigment that was allowed to flow directly from its container onto the support (Fig. 20). It is not visually dissimilar from contemporaneous experiments that were then being conducted by the newest wave of young American painters, the Abstract Expressionists. But the tactile and visual appeal of this current artistic style held little interest for Duchamp, who placed it in the category of art designed primarily for the delectation of the eye, which he called "retinal." It was only when the medium of this work was subjected to forensic analysis some forty years later—long after the death of both Marcel and Maria—that it was discovered to be seminal fluid. Duchamp mounted this strange item into the lid of a valise that he inscribed to Maria in much the way he had signed others for friends: *pour Maria ce no. XII de vingt boîtes-en-valise contenant chacune 69 items et un original et par Marcel Duchamp New York 6 Avril 1946*. The difference between these and all other items that he placed into deluxe valises is that, for the first time, the original item was unique and highly personal, meant for only her to see and understand its significance. Although the expression had not yet come into popular usage, there is no question that, in this particular instance, Duchamp intended for the medium to be its message. He had never made a work of art like this in his entire career, nor, for that matter, had any other artist in history.

Maria certainly understood the privacy of the message, for she did not allow this item to be made public

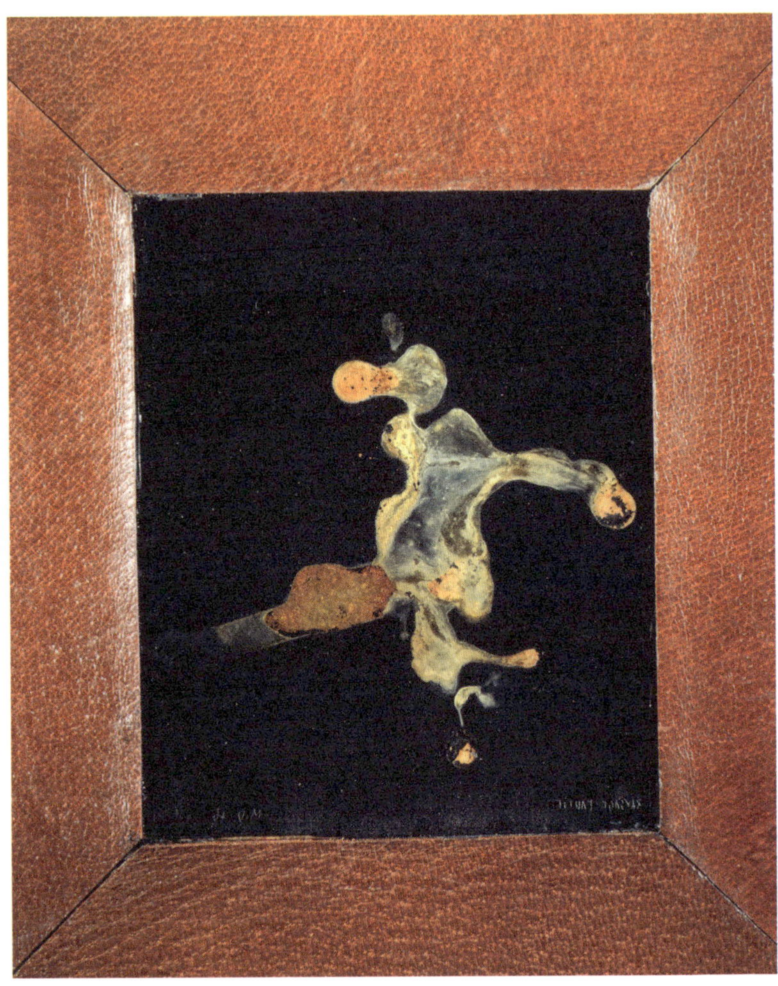

Fig. 20. Marcel Duchamp, *Paysage fautif* (*Faulty Landscape*),
April 1946. Original object mounted into the lid of a deluxe edition of
the *Boîte-en-valise* dedicated to Maria Martins, no. XII/XX. Made
with seminal fluid on Astralon backed with black satin,
8¼ × 6½ in. (21 × 16.5 cm). Museum of Modern Art, Toyama, Japan.

in her lifetime. Maria knew exactly what it was made of, and she certainly understood what it meant: that if Duchamp could not have her physically, then the only possible release of the sexual tension that built up in his body during her absence was through masturbation. For all we know, that very subject might very well have been discussed between them, since they both had a Catholic upbringing and masturbation—which was referred to as "self-abuse" by the church—was considered a mortal sin, which, if not properly confessed and repented, would result in eternal damnation. Neither one of them believed this, of course, since they knew that sexual pleasure—whether self-induced or with a partner—was a perfectly normal and natural aspect of human behavior. In fact, in Duchamp's notes for the *The Large Glass*, onanism or masturbation is one of the main activities given to the Bachelors, who strive to attain union with their bride, only to find that in the end, they miss their mark. Nine holes drilled into the upper portion of the glass are remnants of their splash into her domain. "The bachelor grinds his chocolate himself," Duchamp wrote in his notes, and the spangles of their solidified gas are "hallucinated quite onanistically."

In 1945–46, Duchamp spent much of his time traveling between Maria's apartment on the Upper East Side, Mary Reynolds's apartment in the West Village, and his studio on West 14th Street. "Marcel must have enjoyed [the] vicarious 'home life' which Mary Reynolds gave him and also Maria Martins," Julien Levy recalled years later. "Marcel would happily stay with Maria Martins in her hotel suite in New York in the 1940s and take baths and be looked after for a while, then would disappear down to his 14th Street studio, where she was not allowed to follow him."

In his visits to Maria's studio, one sculpture in particular might have attracted Duchamp's attention, for its title—*Don't Forget I Come from the Tropics* (Fig. 21)—announced the origins of her exotic and emotionally charged sculpture, which could be traced to the same place from which she allegedly came: the wild and largely uncharted territories of the Amazon River basin in Brazil (although in actual fact, it was a place upon which she never set foot). This sculpture features the body of a naked woman lying on her back, her arms outstretched with hands that turn into menacing claws. Her head and legs are missing, but emanating from her torso are five prominent, flamelike projections, a possible allusion to the children Maria had given birth to. (Three were still living, but two had died, one at the age of three and another stillborn.) It is interesting to note that they emanate from the figure's belly and not from her crotch, as if to indicate that these projectiles rise upward from the body without incumbrance, thereby avoiding the pain and suffering usually associated with childbirth. No matter how this work is interpreted, it would lodge itself into the back of Duchamp's mind for some years until he embarked upon a project of his own that involved the depiction of a reclining, naked female figure.

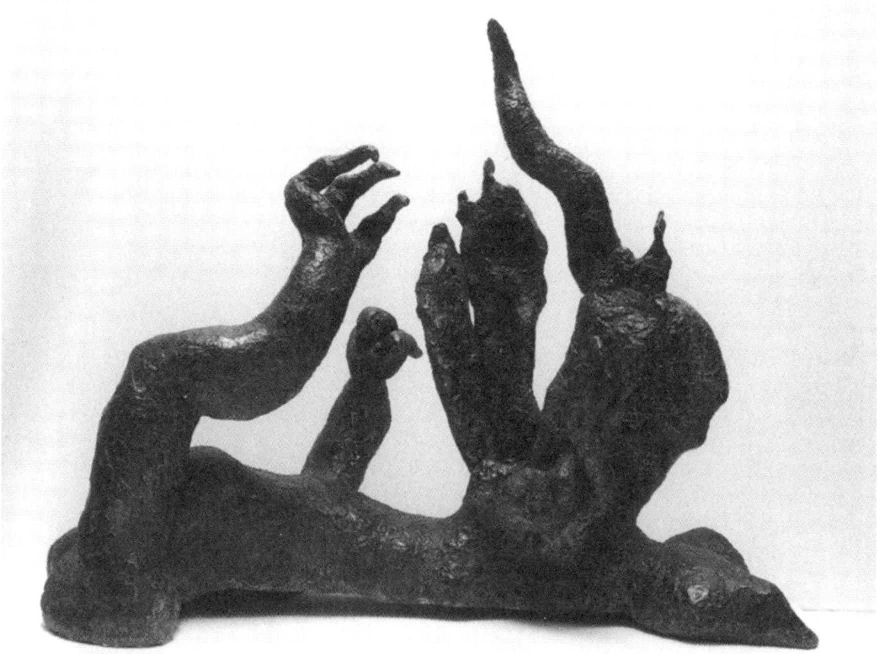

Fig. 21. Maria Martins,
*Don't Forget I Come from the
Tropics*, 1942. Bronze,
$37\frac{3}{8} \times 47\frac{1}{4} \times 27\frac{1}{2}$ in.
(95 × 120 × 69.9 cm).
Formerly collection Sergio
Fadel, Rio de Janeiro.

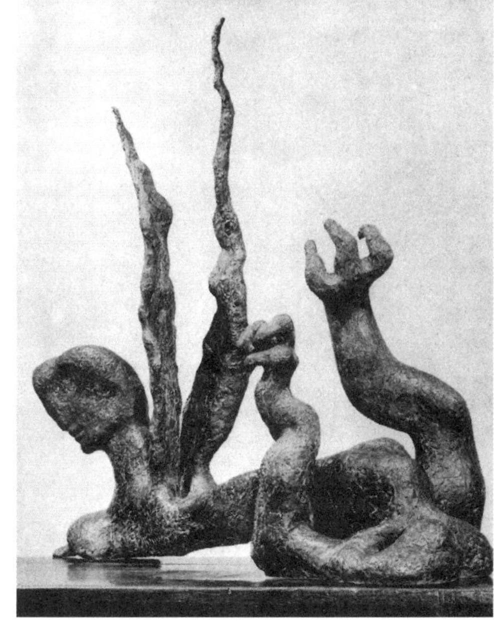

Fig. 22. Maria Martins, *Glèbe-Ailes
(Earthly Wings)*, 1944. Bronze.
Formerly collection Roberto
Marinho, Rio de Janeiro.

BEING

Don't Forget I Come from the Tropics (Fig. 21)—along with ten other more recent sculptures and seven pieces of jewelry—was shown in Maria's fourth and last show at the Valentine Gallery, held in the spring of 1946. The show was called "MARIA: NEW SCULPTURES," and its catalogue listed the works entirely in French, prefaced by a quote from Rainer Maria Rilke's *Letters to a Young Poet*: "Works of art are of an infinite solitude, and no means of approach is so useless as criticism. Only love can touch and hold them and be fair to them." The show was a triumph of Maria's career as a Surrealist sculptor, for the pieces shown in this exhibition represented a significant departure from her earlier work, which was by comparison smaller and more intricate in design. These new sculptures were larger and asserted their presence in the viewer's space in more physically demanding ways. One earlier sculpture called *Glèbe-Ailes* (Earthly Wings), 1944 (Fig. 22), is closely related to *Don't Forget I Come from the Tropics* (Fig. 21). It, too, featured the headless body of a recumbent female figure, but in this case emerging from her pelvic area was a winged head, as if she were giving birth to freedom itself, perhaps an

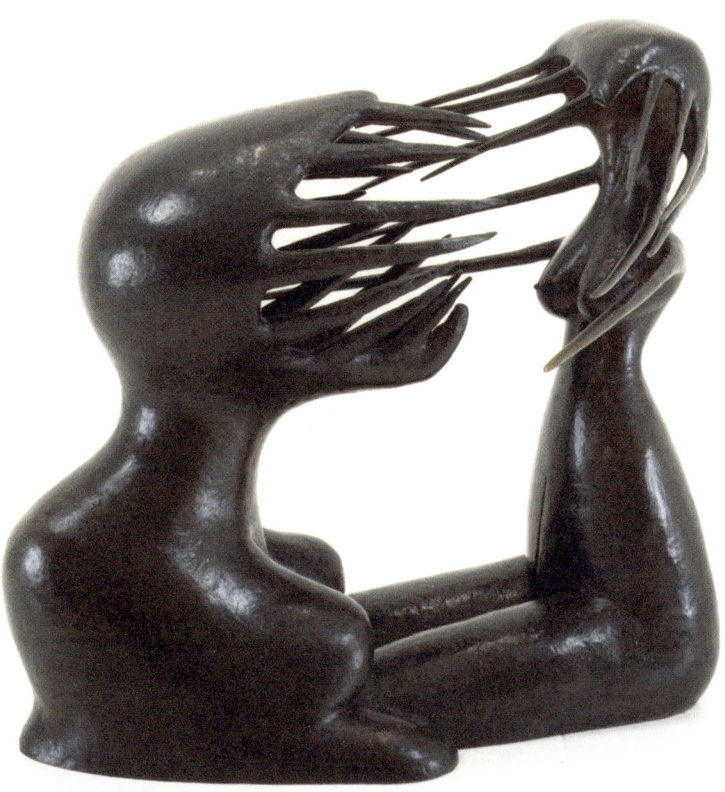

Fig. 23. Maria Martins, *Impossible III*, 1946. Bronze,
31½ × 32½ × 21 in. (80 × 82.6 × 53.3 cm). Museum of
Modern Art, New York; Inter-American Fund, 1946.

oblique reference to the feeling of entrapment Maria felt
when smothered by the desires of men who sought her
affection. If this message was missed in contemplating
the potential meaning of this sculpture, it could not
be so easily avoided when considering the intent of

Impossible, a sculpture Maria produced in no fewer than three variant versions over a two-year period (Figs. 23 and 24).

In all versions of *Impossible*, Maria depicts a male (left) and female (right) figure seemingly locked into perpetual opposition. The heads of both figures are rendered as voids from which project a concentric band of tentacles; the way in which these details are rendered gives each figure a completely different character: the male head resembles a giant jellyfish, while the female looks like a Venus flytrap, the carnivorous tropical plant that snaps its leaves shut in an instant to capture unwary prey. Clearly these two figures are facing an intellectual or cerebral incompatibility: approach the jellyfish too closely and it stings, approach the plant too

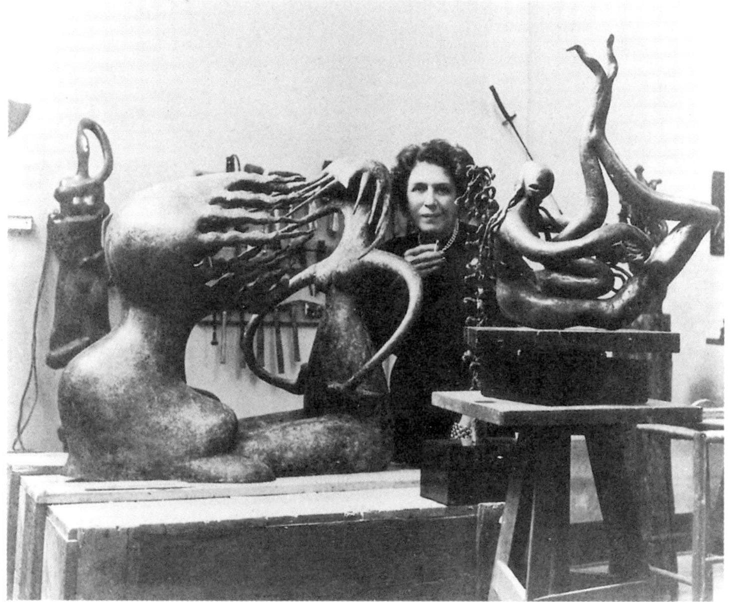

Fig. 24. Maria Martins in her studio, c. 1946, with a version of *Impossible* before her, and her sculpture *Saudade* (Longing), 1944. Collection Ignez Ceglia Simoes, Coconut Grove, Florida.

closely and it devours you. The problem may also have been sexual, for the man's legs straddle those of the woman, while his penis lies flaccid between her thighs. In having selected the title *Impossible* for this sculpture, Maria was unquestionably referring to the impossibility of her relationship with Duchamp. Around the time when she was still working on it, she wrote a poem that, if not directly related to her affair, must have been directed to the various men in her life who fell so easily under her spell. It is worthwhile to read these words with the image of *Impossible* in mind, for only then can we realize why the title she chose for this sculpture was so appropriate:

> *Even long after my death*
> *Long after your death*
> *I want to torture you.*
> *I want the thought of me*
> *to coil around your body like a serpent of fire*
> *without burning you.*
>
> *I want to see you lost, asphyxiated, wander*
> *in the murky haze*
> *woven by my desires.*
>
> *For you, I want long sleepless nights*
> *filled by the roaring tom-tom of storms*
> *Far away, invisible, unknown.*
> *Then, I want the nostalgia of my presence*
> *to paralyze you.*

The variant versions of *Impossible* are most easily distinguished from one another by the position of the arms of the female figure, which at first are placed in the form of a circle but are then reduced in later versions to projecting spikes. Earlier versions of this work can be seen in photographs of Maria taken in her studio (Fig. 24). In the photograph that shows her surrounded by examples of her most recent sculpture (Fig. 10), an example of *Impossible* can be seen next to the window, but we can now see that positioned directly behind her head hangs a framed black-and-white photographic portrait of the individual who, within this context, can be considered her muse: Marcel Duchamp (Fig. 25). There is little doubt that he inspired the making of *Impossible*, for in coded form, it expresses precisely her sentiments about their tortured relationship: no matter what they might have felt for each other, because of her commitment to her husband and children as well as to the diplomatic lifestyle in which she flourished, it was a relationship that was virtually impossible to sustain.

When Maria's show opened at the Valentine Gallery, a finished bronze cast of *Impossible* was not yet available, so she showed the work in the form of an unfinished plaster. In his weekly roundup of reviews for the *New York Times*, Edward Alden Jewell reproduced the plaster, and expressed some relief in observing that Maria had finally departed from her earlier reliance upon themes drawn from her native Brazil. "There was a time when it looked as if the Brazilian jungle, whence her idiom derives, might smother even so energetic and dynamic a sculptor," he wrote. "Now it is generally under control. The strange, contorted forms are in the main much more clearly plastic. And completely, intricately riddled with arcana, they hint, often, at grave meanings related to the dilemma of a post-war

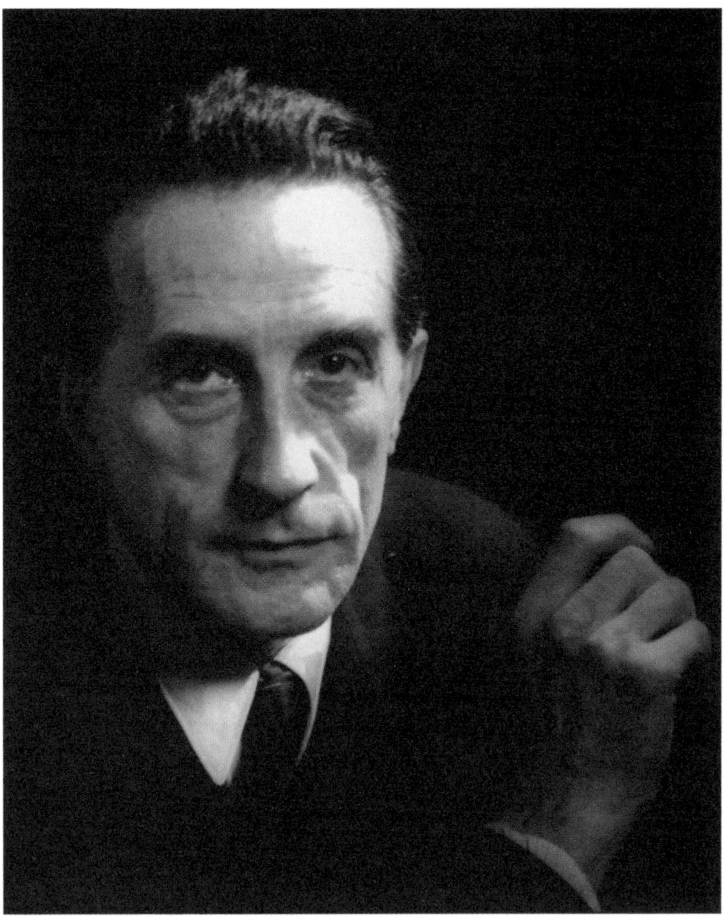

Fig. 25. Ethel Pries, *Portrait of Marcel Duchamp*, 1946.
Private collection, Paris.

world—a dilacerating dilemma, primordial, yet charged with an immediacy urgent and ominous."

Impossible was also reproduced in a notice about the exhibition that appeared in *Time* magazine, where the reporter described the work as "Maria's most startling

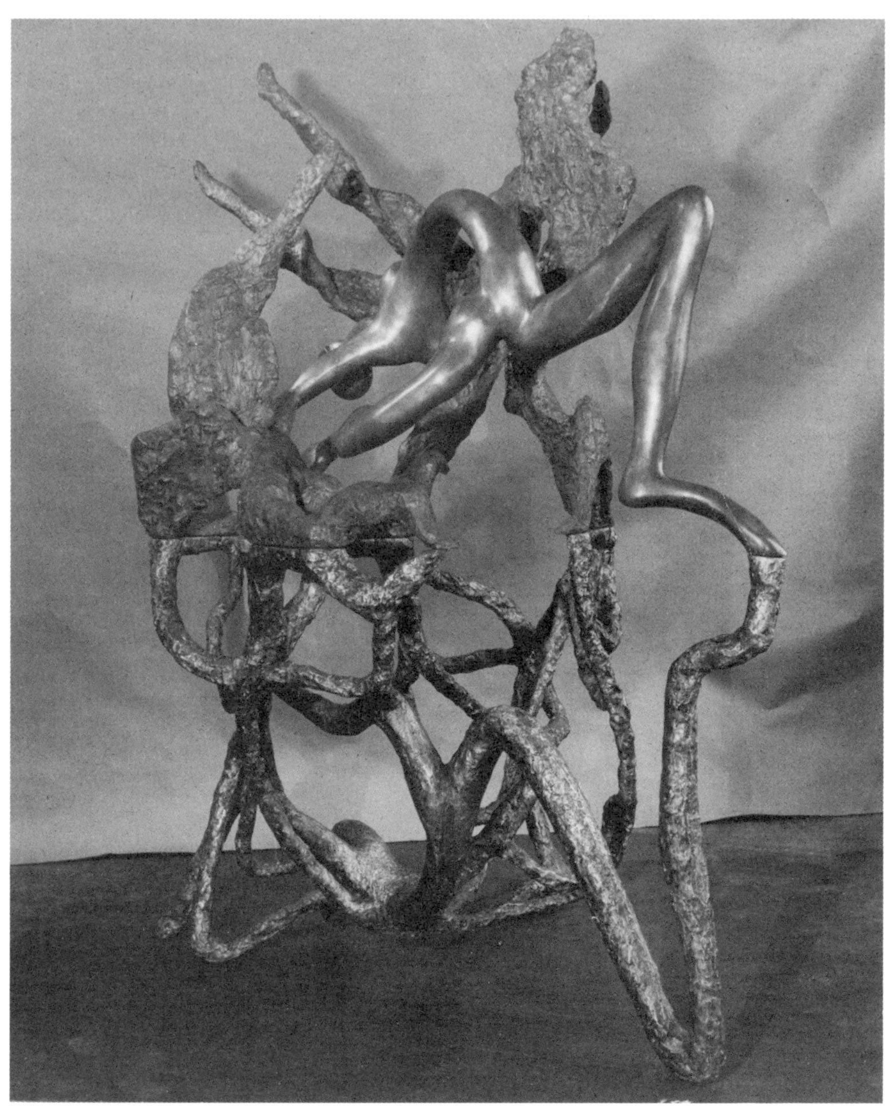

Fig. 26. Maria Martins, *Je crus avoir longuement rêvé que j'étais libre*
(I Believed That I Long Dreamed I Was Free), 1946. Bronze, 69 × 64 in.
(175.3 × 162.6 cm). Photograph of the sculpture at the Davis Museum of Art at
Wellesley College, Wellesley, Massachusetts. Now mostly lost or destroyed.

Fig. 26a. Detail on opposite page.

new effort," which, he said, "looked like a disagreement between two anthropomorphic snowstorms." He confessed, however, that the artist had a less literal interpretation. "The world is complicated and sad," she is quoted as having said. "It is nearly impossible to make people understand each other." She also told the reporter that "art is the underground of the world, and we will win in the end." The statement was remarkably prescient, for not only does it accurately describe the course of Maria's future artistic reputation, but it also echoes a position that Duchamp established in this period pertaining to his own work. Indeed, it was in this very year—1946—that he began work on an elaborate environmental construction that he worked on in secrecy for the next twenty years. From now on, he would work underground, away from the watchful eyes of critics and even close friends, a firm and unaltering commitment that he made to Maria and to himself.

The single most important sculpture by Maria included in the Valentine Gallery show went curiously

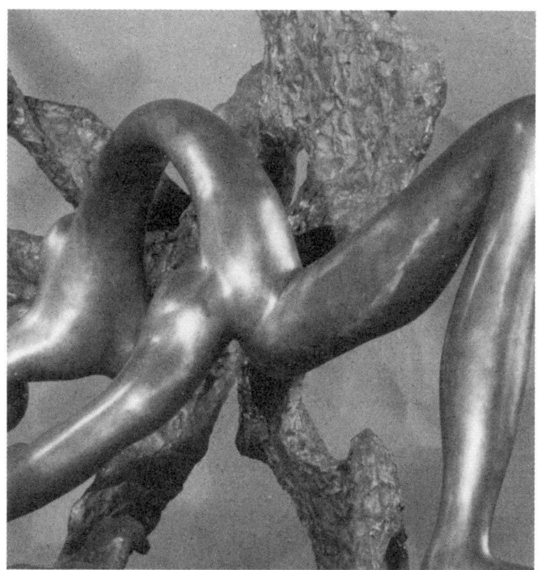

unmentioned by the critics, but there is some evidence that it did not go unnoticed by Duchamp. *Je crus avoir longuement revé que j'étais libre* (I Believed That I Long Dreamed I Was Free; Fig. 26) was a monumental sculpture measuring nearly six feet in height that depicted a nude female figure entrapped within vegetation, her head arching back and out of view, but her distended pelvic area thrown directly in the face of the viewer (Fig. 26a). Closer examination reveals that the figure—distinguished from the rest of the sculpture by being made of polished bronze—is embedded within a dense thicket of vegetation growing in a riverbed, while the lower portion (divided by an invisible horizonal plane that runs through the center of the sculpture) represents its distorted reflection in the moving water and undergrowth seen below. Although this sculpture was subsequently destroyed and is known today in only fragmentary form, it could be argued that—in three dimensions—it represents a unique and powerful expression of abstraction that would find its only parallel in the paintings of artists like Willem de Kooning, Franz Kline and Jackson Pollock (who had earlier professed a preference for sculpture over painting and never abandoned his desire to someday be recognized as a great sculptor).

In conjunction with the show, the Valentine Gallery published a lavish, limited-edition portfolio of engravings by Maria. In the mid-1940s, Maria had taken classes in printmaking at Atelier 17, a workshop run by the English artist Stanley William Hayter. During the years of World War II, Atelier 17 moved from Paris to temporary quarters provided by the New School for Social Research in New York. Hayter was known as printmaker to the Surrealists, and, by the mid-1930s he had already learned "to give surreal effects of transparency to his images," as an art historian recently observed, "by rubbing coarse carborundum across the engraved plate, then rubbing out with a burnisher to lighten a figure yet leave it merged with the ground." This technique accurately describes the process used by Maria to create four of the engravings included in the Valentine Gallery portfolio (Fig. 27a–d), where she elected to depict examples of her sculpture enveloped by the dense black ink ground of the printing plate. There was even a rendition of *Impossible* (Fig. 27c), where the male and female figures seem to be quarreling with one another, their tentacles clashing in a blur of frenzied combat. Maria pulled these engravings herself, on a small press that she set up in a room adjacent to her studio (Fig. 28).

The Valentine Gallery portfolio also included four engravings reproducing the handwritten text of a three-part prose poem by Maria in French, entitled "Explication" (first page: Fig. 27b). The words of the poem are addressed forcefully to a specific individual whose identity is not disclosed, but, knowing of Maria's intense relationship with Duchamp at the time, it is difficult not to think she had him in mind. When read aloud, the poem reads like a literary metaphor of the art of lovemaking, beginning with foreplay and ending in orgasm. The cadence slowly builds through the first two stanzas, evoking tranquil scenes of the tropical night and rustling leaves. But in the last section, the mood suddenly quickens, the wind runs "to a lofty frenzy" and "is singing and moaning the great song of strength and desire." Trees then "offer themselves giving and taking,

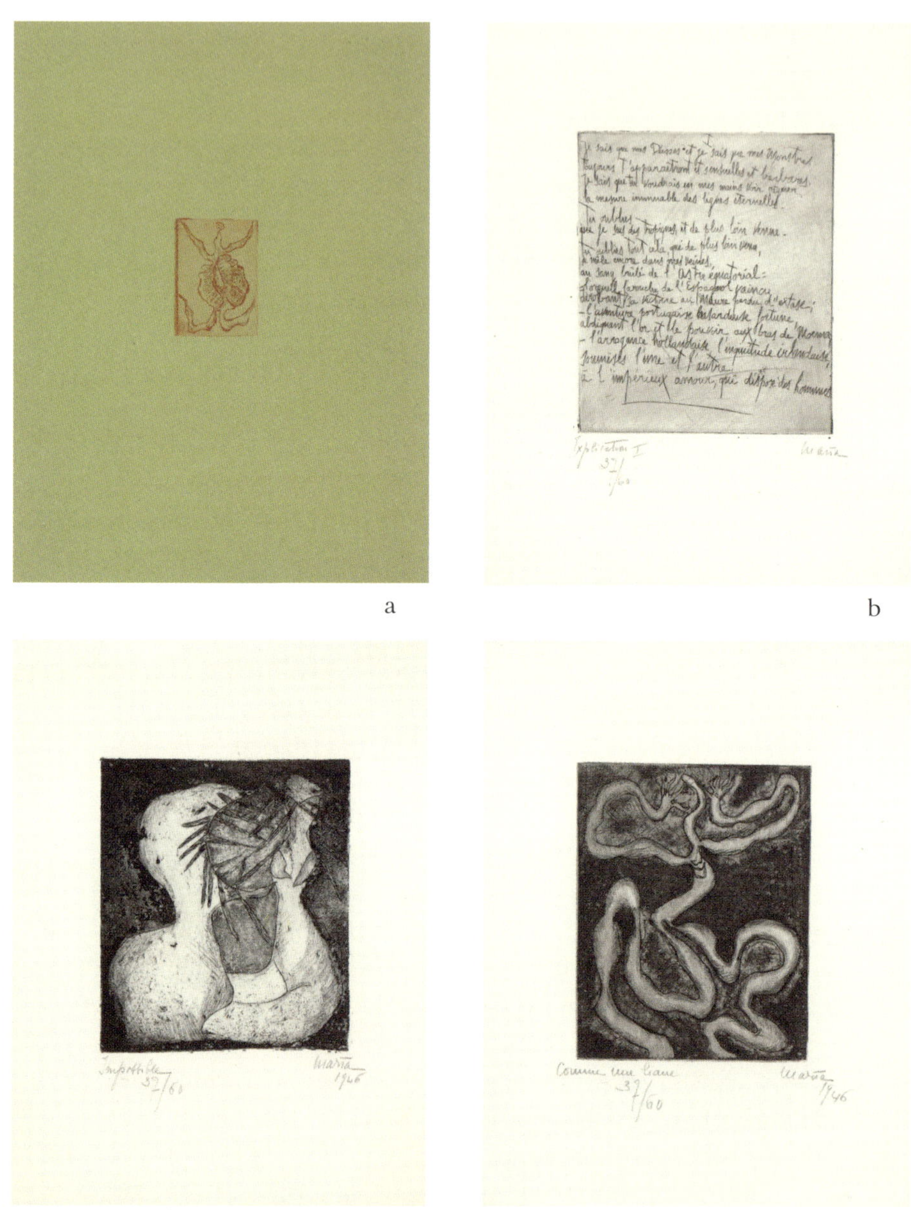

Fig. 27a–d. Maria Martins, *Maria*, portfolio of etchings published by
Valentine Gallery, New York, 1946. Edition of 60 signed and numbered copies;
each page 14⅜ × 11¼ in. (36.5 × 28.6 cm). Museum of Modern Art,
New York; gift of Mr. and Mrs. Alfred H. Barr, Jr.

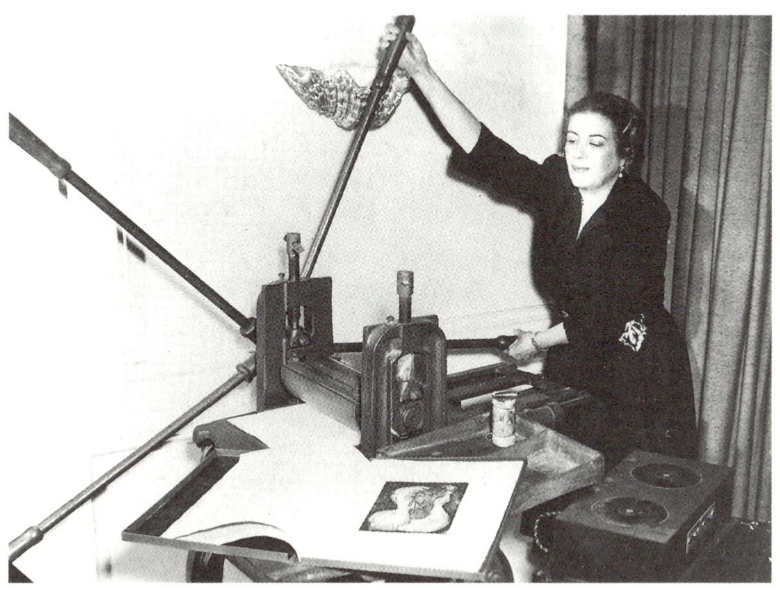

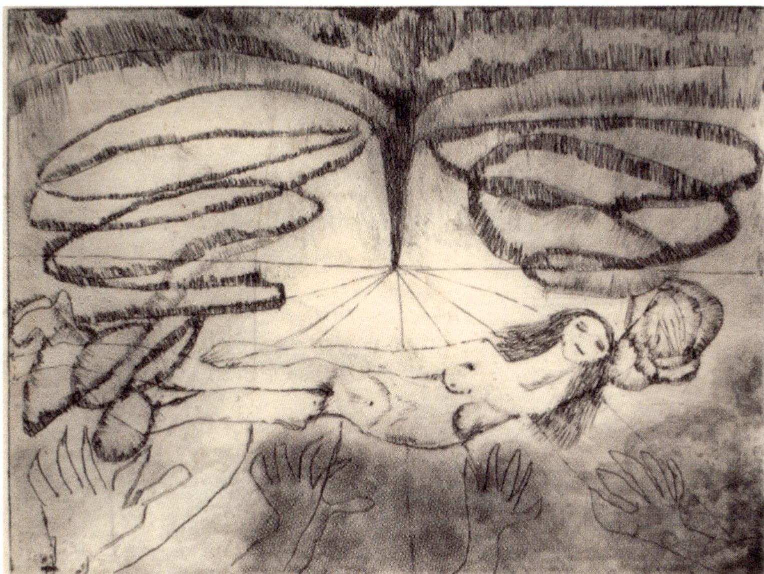

Fig. 28. Maria Martins using the printing press
in her New York studio, c. 1946.

Fig. 29. Maria Martins, *Untitled*, c. 1946. Etching,
12⅕ × 8¼ in. (31 × 21 cm).

taking and giving, until their coupling has reached the height of exhaustion," whereupon in an instant "everything returns to its initial tranquility, painfully reborn in the conquest of fulfillment."

Not included in the Valentine portfolio but likely produced at around this same time is an untitled engraving by Maria that depicts a nude female figure lying on her back (Fig. 29), an image that has no precedent in her earlier work but forms a compelling comparison with the ambitious project Duchamp had in mind that would serve as an homage to the woman he loved. In the engraving, the figure lies recumbent in a space defined by perspective lines that converge in the distance at a point that erupts into a tornado, which splits into two dark spiraling forms that envelop the entire upper half of the image. Hands with sharp fingertips seem to claw at her body from below, while, judging from the lack of expression on her face, she lies on the ground oblivious to her surroundings. Most significant for the work Duchamp was thinking about, she holds in her outstretched left hand some sort of object that is difficult to make out. Graça Ramos—one of the foremost authorities on Maria's work in Brazil—thought this figure related to the legends of Yara and felt that what she held in her hand might be "a mirror, a lamp, a comb, or a flower," but she was uncertain. To my mind it looks like a glowing gas lamp enveloped by the swirling lines of the tornado, just as its twin forms on the other side of the image seem to break their pattern and enter the space between the figure's outstretched legs. "She is nude, her eyes closed, with long hair," Ramos poignantly observed. "Her legs are intertwined and her genital region, covered with hair, is visible."

CONSUMMATION
& CONCEPTION

Whenever Duchamp was without Maria for extended periods, he wrote letters to her, some of which are heartbreaking in their sadness, as they are being written by a man who has fallen completely and desperately in love with a woman who cannot express her commitment to him exclusively. "Despite everything you tell yourself," he writes in a moment of acute loneliness in an effort to rationalize the condition of his solitude, "I actually like being alone here in the studio. But there is room enough for two if you want to be as one with my freedom, and a greater freedom still will come of it, as yours will protect and foster mine, and mine yours, I hope." He openly pours out his heart in an effort to assess their situation. "You must know me well enough by now to realize that for the first time in my life I find myself accepting you completely as you are, without any feeling of rebellion of any kind, and that it has at last been granted to me to love you simply and purely, i.e., without the vaudeville farce that generally accompanies the trials and tribulations of two lovers." In joining him, he does not believe she will lose anything. "It is also essential that our individuality be always in harmony, and that we avoid the mundane exchanges of conjugal antagonism (not at all necessary)." He signs the letter simply "M."

A month after Duchamp gave Maria his valise containing a landscape made with his seminal fluid (Fig. 20), he traveled to Paris, where he visited various family members, met old friends, and negotiated on behalf of the Museum of Modern Art in New York to acquire important works by European modernists. He sailed, ironically, on a ship called the SS *Brazil*, which left New York on May 1, 1946. As soon as he arrived, he wrote to Maria in New York telling her that he is "in a state of terrible depression," but that he anxiously awaits her arrival, which he expects will be in a few weeks. After updating her on the conditions in Paris after the war, he says, "I have not yet detected the slightest echo, not even an imperceptive one, of our love, which seems not to have filtered out to an unwanted public," ending *Je t'adore* (I love you). When Maria arrived, Duchamp introduced her to his good friend Henri-Pierre Roché, one of the few people in Paris whom he trusted completely and who would not circulate the information in the art world that he was having an affair with a married woman.

During his meeting with Maria, Duchamp gave her a deluxe copy of his *Green Box* (Figs. 30 through 33), one likely left at his apartment on the rue Larrey, which he continued to rent but had been occupied in his absence by members of the French Resistance. This particular example of the box contained his first sketch for *The Large Glass* which he inscribed "*pour Maria, enfin arrivée*" (Fig. 32). There is no question that Duchamp was informing Maria that in no uncertain terms she was his *Mariée*, the Bride of *The Large Glass* that he desired

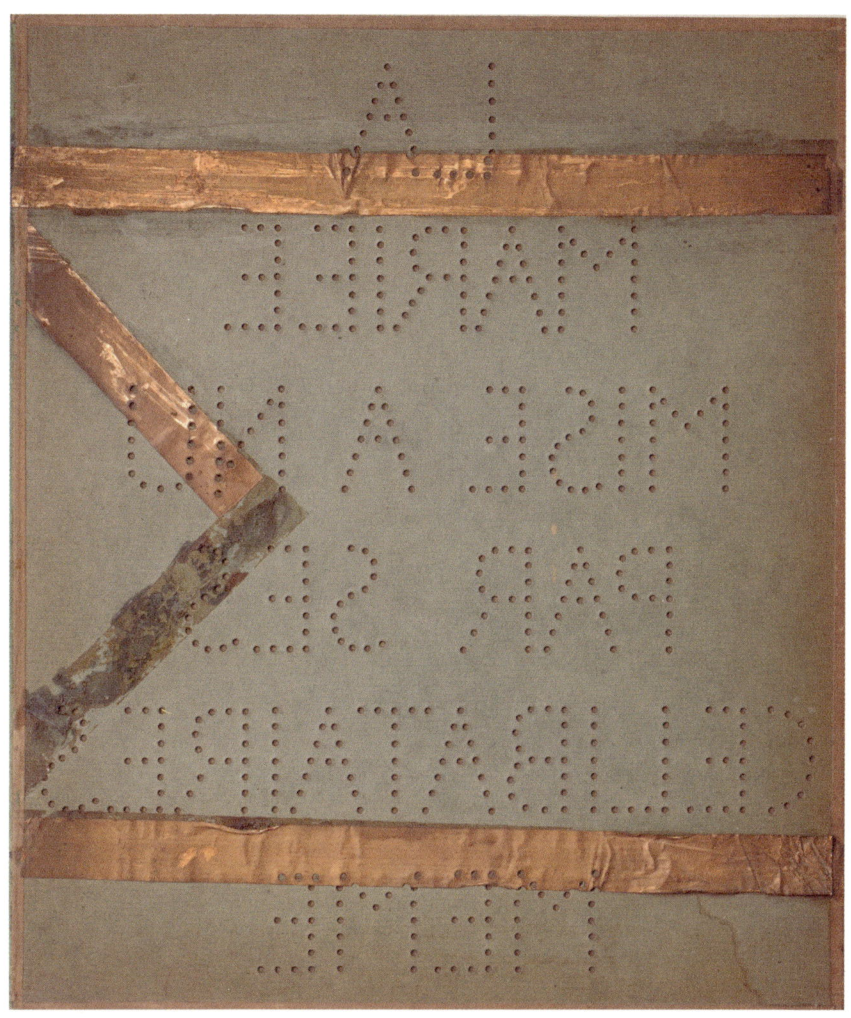

Fig. 30. Marcel Duchamp, *La Mariée mis à nu par ses célibataires, même* (The Bride Stripped Bare by Her Bachelors, Even), or *La Boîte Verte* (The Green Box), 1934. Cover. San Francisco Museum of Modern Art.

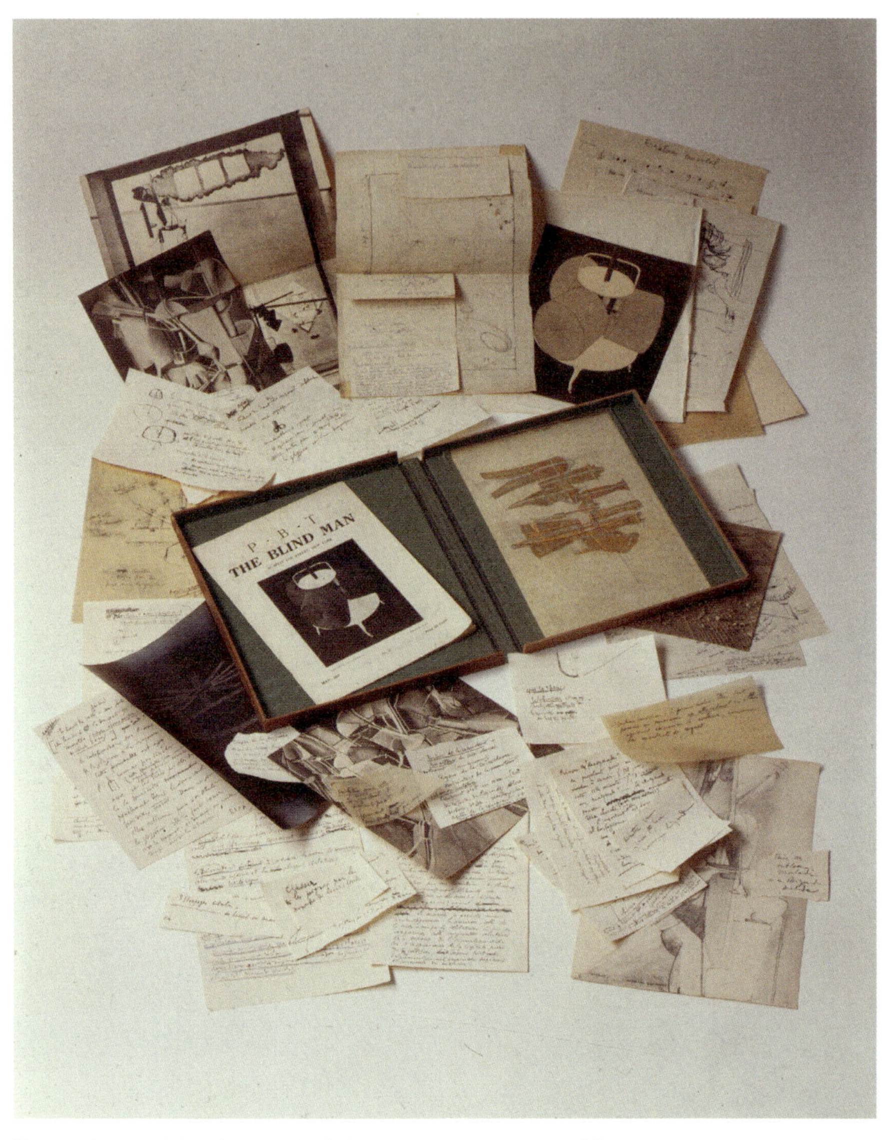

Fig. 31. Marcel Duchamp, *La Mariée mis à nu par ses célibataires, même* (The Bride Stripped Bare by Her Bachelors, Even), or *La Boîte Verte* (The Green Box), 1934. Contents open for display. San Francisco Museum of Modern Art.

more than thirty years earlier, but who had finally arrived in his life. At least one Duchamp scholar has suggested that the word *arrivée* might also refer to sexual climax, an intriguing thought that would not have eluded Maria. Indeed, attached to the sketch was a series of notes that related thematically to his *Paysage fautif* (Fig. 20), as they dealt entirely with the liquefaction of Illuminating Gas, that vaporous substance that took on the shape of the Bachelors and solidified, as Duchamp says, "through the phenomenon of stretching in the unit of lengths" as it entered the "capillary tubes," nine lines clearly visible on the surface of the glass emanating from the midsections or points of discharge, which Duchamp labeled in a perspective study for the Bachelors "the plane of sex."

To get an idea of what Duchamp might have found so intimate about this note—which one Duchamp scholar later described as "a coded love letter"—we need only analyze its contents. The scientific terms that Duchamp uses, as well as the diagrams that accompany them, are a thinly disguised anatomy lesson, but in this case, one for a mechanized bachelor who, nonetheless, like his human counterpart, is equipped with internal organs and tubes designed to transport erotic liquids through his body. The Bachelors, Duchamp writes, "respond to all of the questions of love with a sparkling brutality," their "inaccessible request" responded to only by a mirror that reflects "back to them their own complexity, deluding them fairly onanistically." Since they cannot attain immediate satisfaction from the Bride (the liquefaction process is doubtless a metaphor for the production of semen), they must seek at least temporary relief from their sexual frustrations

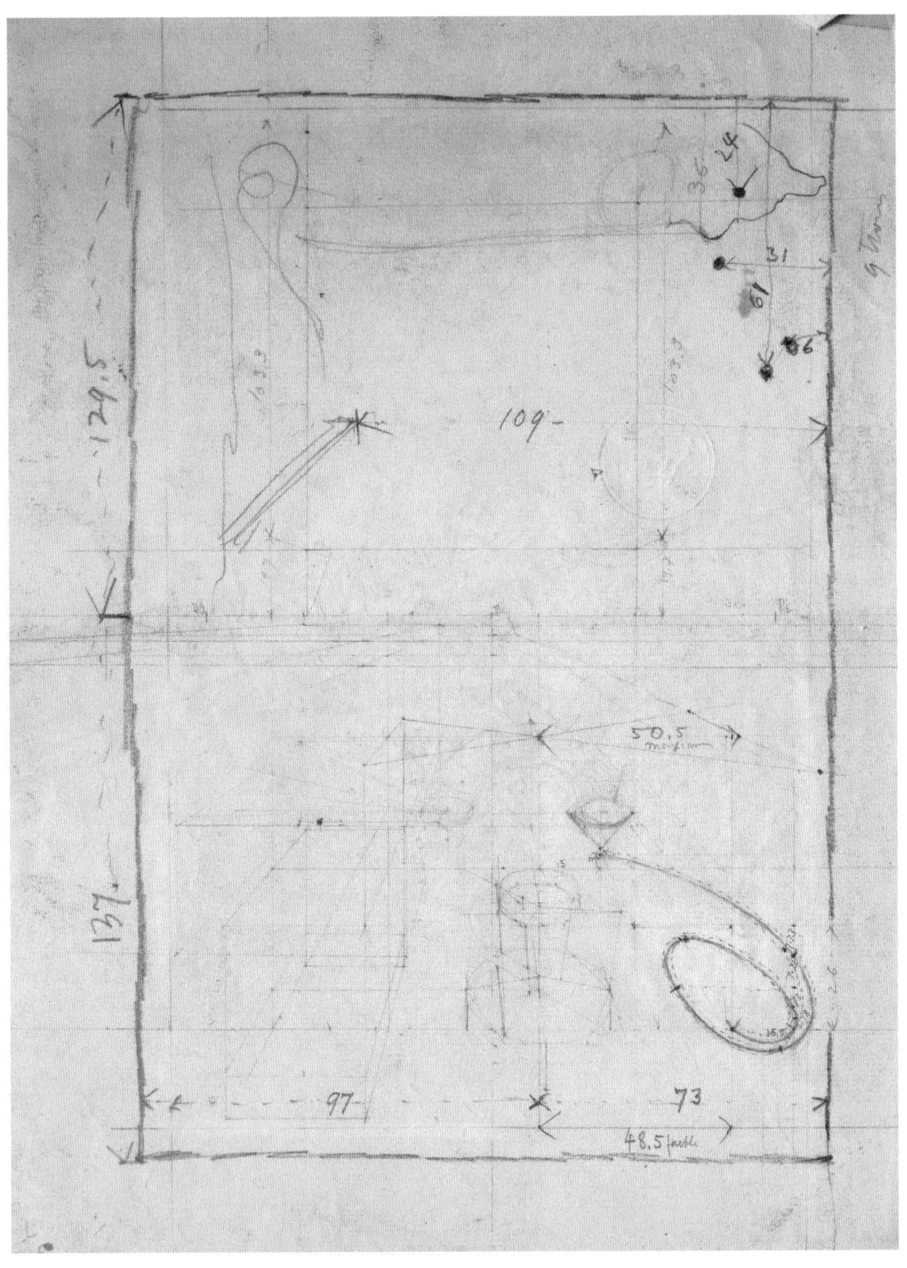

Fig. 32. Marcel Duchamp, first preparatory sketch for
La Mariée mis à nu par ses célibataires, même (The Bride Stripped Bare by
Her Bachelors, Even), 1913. San Francisco Museum of Modern Art.

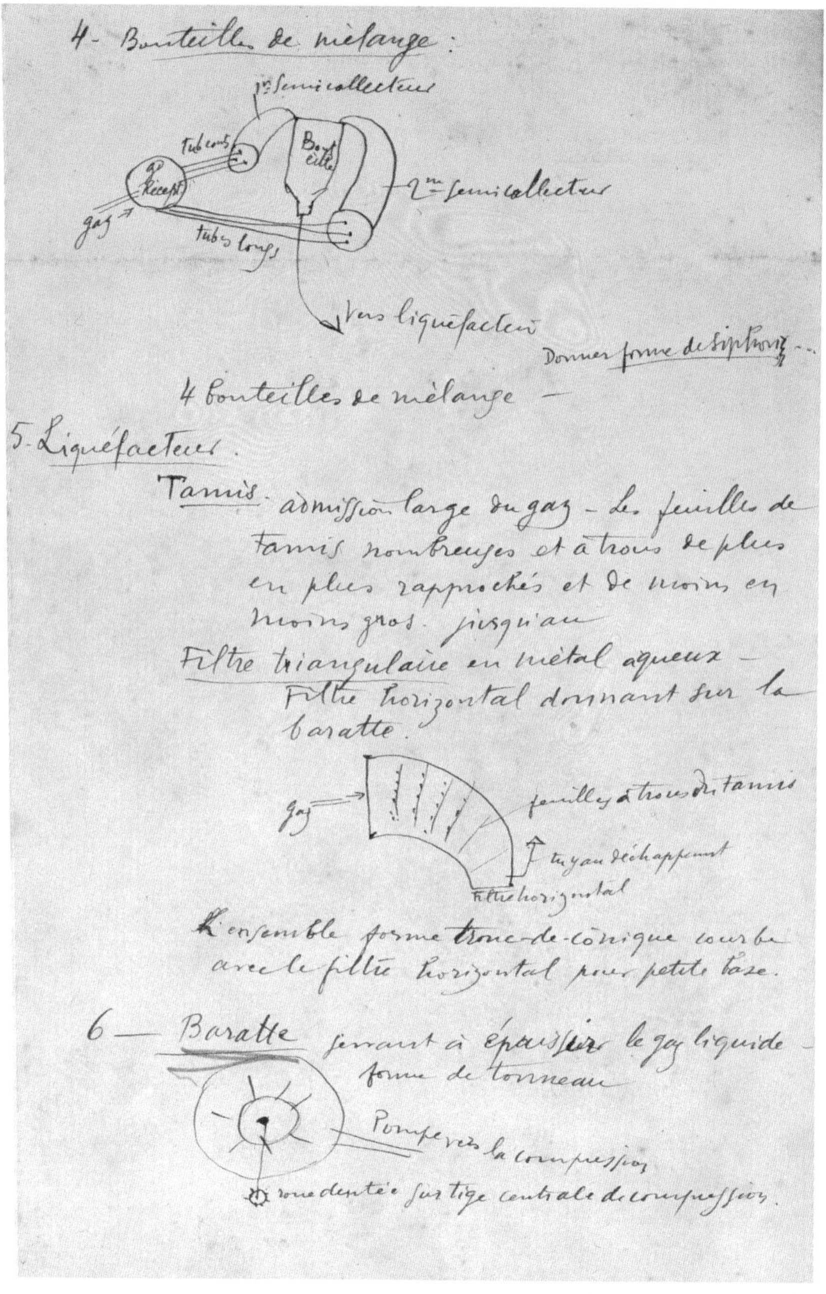

4 - Bouteille de mélange :

1er Semi-collecteur

Tub courts

Récept

gaz

Bouteille

2me Semi-collecteur

tubs longs

vers liquéfacteur

Donner forme de siphon —

4 bouteilles de mélange —

5. Liquéfacteur.

Tamis. admission large du gaz — Les feuilles de tamis nombreuses et à trous de plus en plus rapprochés et de moins en moins gros. jusqu'au

Filtre triangulaire en métal aqueux — Filtre horizontal donnant sur la baratte.

gaz

feuilles à trous du tamis

tuyau d'échappement

Filtre horizontal

L'ensemble forme tronc-de-cônique courbe avec le filtre horizontal pour petite base.

6 — Baratte servant à épaissir le gaz liquide — forme de tonneau

Pompe vers la compression

roue dentée sur tige centrale de compression.

Fig. 33. Marcel Duchamp, note on the liquefaction of gas in *The Large Glass*, 1913. San Francisco Museum of Modern Art.

without any assistance from her. On the last page of this note (Fig. 33), Duchamp visualizes three mechanical devices that facilitate the liquefaction process: a triturator, a condenser, and a churn. Of the three elements, the triturator—which, traditionally, is a mechanism used to pulverize a solid in order to enhance its solution in a liquid—is the most erotically charged. It closely resembles a diagram of the male reproductive organs and, more specifically, one that traces the flow of semen from the testes to the penis, represented metaphorically by an inverted bottle from which emerges an arrow labeled *vers liquéfacteur*, which can be translated as "toward condenser." The condenser is, basically, a filter, which at this point Duchamp describes as being triangular in shape and consisting of separate sheets punctured with holes that become increasingly smaller in size. In order to draw the liquid through the condenser, Duchamp devises a *baratte*, or churn, which rotates and creates suction, thereby helping to draw the liquid through the filter.

Duchamp's presentation of this note to Maria would have given him the ideal opportunity to describe how he had used the fourth dimension as a means by which to convey to viewers the ultimate unification of his Bride with her Bachelors—that is to say, a means by which to render the sensation of orgasm. The fourth dimension was a concept that mathematicians had speculated about for more than half a century, but which artists found especially intriguing because they were limited to working in only three. A number of them speculated that the fourth dimension was a conceptual realm in which they operated that transcended the confines of our natural world. Since the Bride is rendered in two dimensions, the Bachelors in three, the fourth was reserved for their ultimate unification, which Duchamp elected to render visible through the science of optics. This part of *The Large Glass* was only discussed in the notes and left unrealized when the project was abandoned and left intentionally incomplete. The sudden discharge of sexual tension that occurs in orgasm is a phenomenon that is difficult to describe for both males and females—except to say that rhythmic muscular contractions seem to be confined to the pelvic area—so one can only imagine how difficult it would be to render visible. Duchamp believed that such a pleasurable sensation must take place in a realm that existed beyond the confines of our natural world, in a fourth dimension that could only be referred to in metaphorical terms, in his case through the science of optics. "The erotic act," he later explained, was "the fourth dimensional situation par excellence." The very discussion of this subject between two sexually consenting adults was the sort of subtle verbal foreplay in which we can only imagine Marcel and Maria willingly engaged.

It is natural to wonder what the consummation of their affections entailed. Maria's daughter, Nora, actually thought their relationship might have been "more cerebral than physical" (although she added, "my mother would be furious to hear me say that"). If Maria's prior affair with Lipchitz is any indication, she probably treated the act of making love as a wild and uninhibited event, entrapping her men as a Venus flytrap consumes its prey, much like the female figure in her sculpture *Impossible* (Fig. 23). Moreover, as the poem that is associated with this sculpture suggests, she wanted the "nostalgia of her presence" to "paralyze" the men with whom she became romantically involved. Duchamp, on the other hand, was always the consummate gentleman, "as gentle in bed," as Beatrice Wood (a former lover) recalled, "as he was out of it." A more appropriate and fitting tribute to a man's care and sensitivity toward the woman he loves is hard to imagine.

It was likely that around this time—in the mid-1940s, when Duchamp's affair with Maria had reached a dramatic crescendo—that he would render visible elements within *The Large Glass* that were essential components of its design, but that were unseen and existed—at least insofar as we know—only in his head. These ideas came to him as he was working out the various components of the glass, and are outlined in a note that begins *Étant donnés: 1° la chute d'eau / 2° le gaz d'éclairage* (Given: 1° the waterfall / 2° the illuminating gas). Basically, what this note tells us is that these two components—water and gas—are "given" (the word used in the same sense as in a mathematical theorem), that is to say, they already exist as essential components of the design and are so obvious as to not require the necessity of making them visible. Besides, they are both transparent substances and rendering them on the surface of glass would be superfluous, but they were doubtless in the back of his mind as he spent nearly three years working out the intricate details of his elaborate lovemaking machine (plus an additional eight years devoted to its actual execution). There was of course another component to the glass that was visible only in abstract form—the Bride herself, rendered in the form of entangled, overlapping visceral forms both in a painting and in the upper section of *The Large Glass*—but which now, with Maria in his life, had become visually manifest.

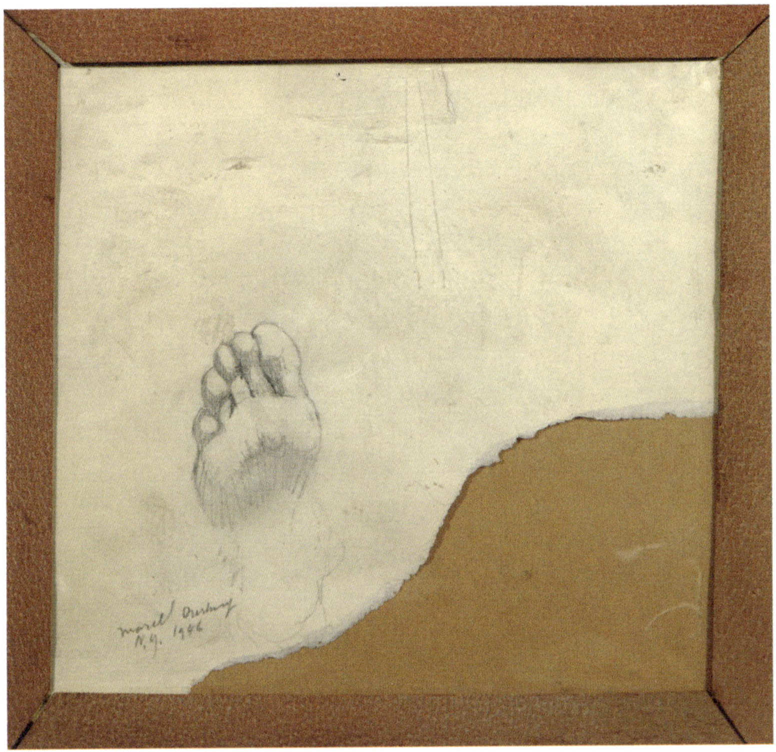

Fig. 34. Marcel Duchamp, *Untitled* (*Underside of a Foot*),
1946. Pencil on paper, drawing mounted into the lid of a
Boîte-en-valise. Artizon Museum, Tokyo.

He likely devoted some thought as to how all three of
these elements—the water, gas, and Maria—could be
made visible, and exactly what form that would take.

It could have been in a Paris hotel, or possibly earlier in his New York studio, that Duchamp conveyed
some of these ideas to Maria, and asked if she would
consider posing nude for him. She likely agreed with no
hesitation, so he asked her to remove her clothing and
lie down, possibly on a bed or platform where he could

sit in a chair and view her reclining body straight-on. For all we know, he might have had in mind the engraving Maria made of a nude, recumbent female figure holding some sort of object in her hand (Fig. 29), but for now, he wanted to begin with a drawing of her body. Seeing her from below in this supine position proved compelling, so he likely just began drawing. The first detail of her anatomy that came into view was the underside of her foot, which he drew in an acutely naturalistic fashion (Fig. 34). This would have been an unusual point from which to view a figure, one rendered so rarely in the history of art that what might come to mind for most art historians is the famous *Dead Christ* by Andrea Mantegna in the Brera Picture Gallery in Milan (Fig. 35). A masterpiece like this from the Italian Renaissance might not have occurred to either artist, for a more immediate precedent could be found in Ingres's *Oedipus and the Sphinx* (Fig. 36), a large painting that hung in the Louvre, where the underside of a dead person's foot is visible in the lower-left corner of the picture, clearly a hapless victim who was unable to answer the riddle of the sphinx correctly. The viewpoint Duchamp adopts for Maria in his drawing is close to a diagram that Albrecht Dürer made to illustrate the science of perspective, wherein an artist keeps his eye at a fixed point (at the summit of an obelisk) so that he can draw the body of a reclining female nude in proper foreshortening (Fig. 37).

If the rest of Duchamp's sketch were completed, right behind that foot would be the image of Maria's vulva, something Duchamp chose not to depict in this drawing, nor, for that matter, did he render visible any other detail of her anatomy. Once this image was fixed

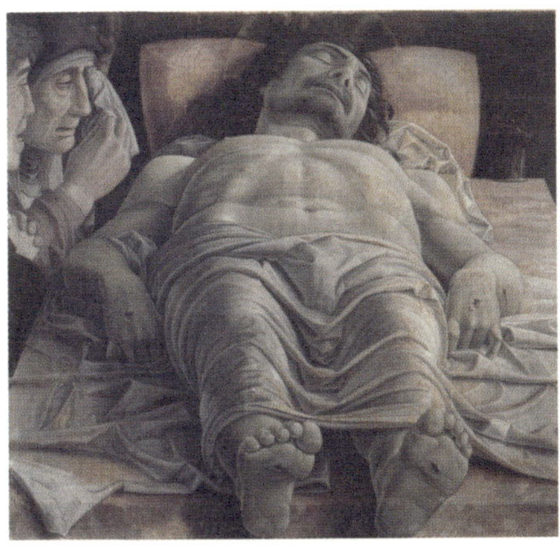

Fig. 35. Andrea Mantegna, *Dead Christ*, 1475–78. Oil and tempera on canvas, 31⅞ × 26¾ in. (81 × 68 cm). Palazzo Brera, Milan.

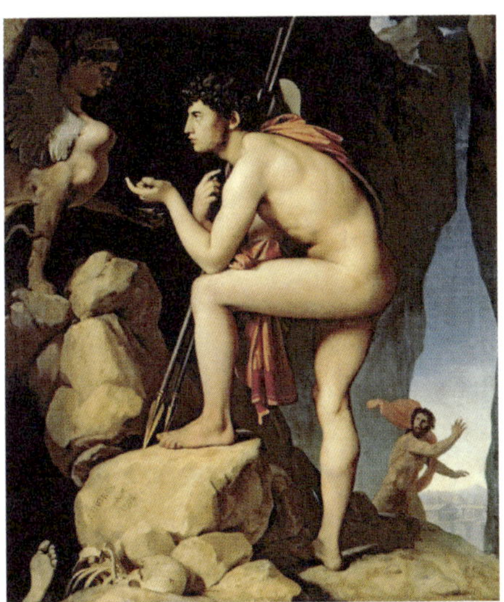

Fig. 36. Jean-Auguste-Dominique Ingres, *Oedipus and the Sphinx*, 1808–27. Oil on canvas, 74½ × 56⅝ in. (189 × 144 cm). Musée du Louvre, Paris

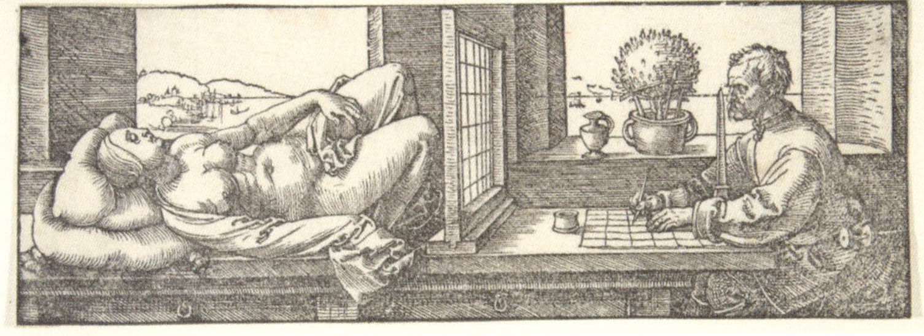

Fig. 37. Albrecht Dürer, *Draughtsman Making a Perspective Drawing of a Reclining Woman*, c. 1600. Woodcut, 3 × 87½ (7.7 × 21.4 cm). Metropolitan Museum of Art; gift of Henry Walters

in his mind, however, there is yet another precedent in the history of art that was not then commonly available for view, but which most artists knew about: Gustave Courbet's *Origin of the World* (Fig. 38), the provocative, close-up view of a woman's naked crotch and little else. At the time, the painting was still in a private collection in Paris, but most artists knew about its existence, as the subject was sufficiently notorious as to be infamous. For the time being, the portrayal of a nude female figure from such a dramatic position was held in abeyance, but Duchamp would come back to it within a year, when he and Maria began seeing each other on a regular basis in New York to work together on the execution of details pertaining to the elaborate work he envisioned.

Maria remained in Paris for only about a month, returning to Washington, DC, on a flight accompanied by Henri-Pierre Roché. Two weeks later, Duchamp embarked upon a vacation to Switzerland with Mary Reynolds, who had been invited to visit her close friends, Hélène and Henri Hoppenot, French ambassador to Switzerland. For a few days they were guests at the Hoppenots' palatial residence in Bern, but later they checked into the Hôtel Bellevue in Chexbres, about an hour and a half south by train on the shores of Lake Geneva (Lac Léman in French). The hotel was recommended by Hélène Hoppenot, who had stayed there with her family as a child. Their rooms overlooked the lake, but Marcel became fascinated with a nearby waterfall called Le Forestay, which he thought might form the ideal backdrop for the project he was working on with Maria. He took several pictures of the coursing waters as they cascaded down the hill in a deep ravine nestled

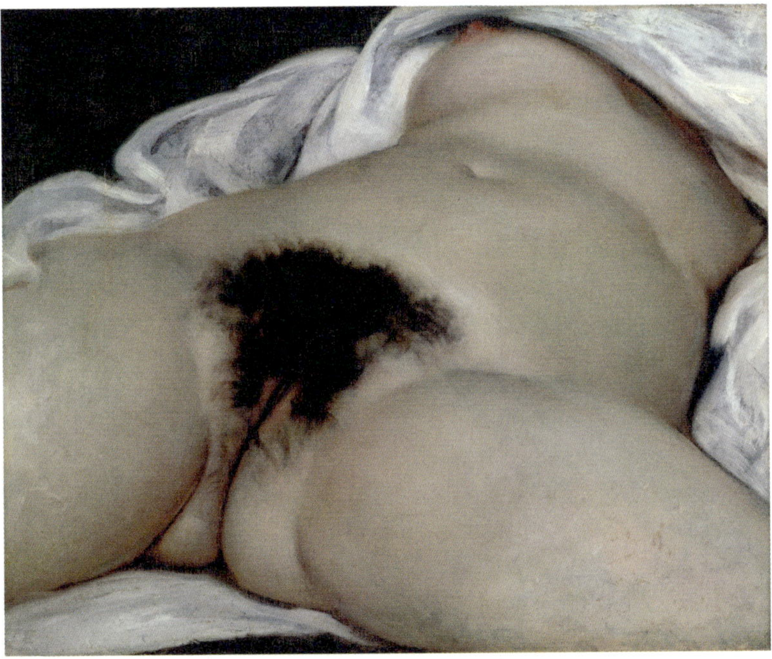

Fig. 38. Gustave Courbet, *L'Origine du Monde* (Origin of the World), 1866. Oil on canvas, 18 × 22 in. (46 × 55 cm). Musée d' Orsay, Paris.

between houses and into the nearby lake (Fig. 39). At some point during the course of the year that followed, Duchamp told Mary about his relationship with Maria, and probably confessed that he was in love with her. Mary, in turn, relayed this information to her friend Hélène, who wrote in her diary: "Mary herself is hardly cheerful, and I sense that her instability derives from what she calls 'Marcel's desertion.' . . . She has learned that Marcel has been seeing a lot of Maria Martins. . . . I tell her: 'I don't think that she presents a great danger to you.'" Hélène then goes on to suggest why she felt Duchamp was so enamored of this woman, which she considered a case of opposites attracting. "I think to myself that it is [Maria's] extreme animalism that attracts the one-hundred-percent intellectual who is Marcel Duchamp."

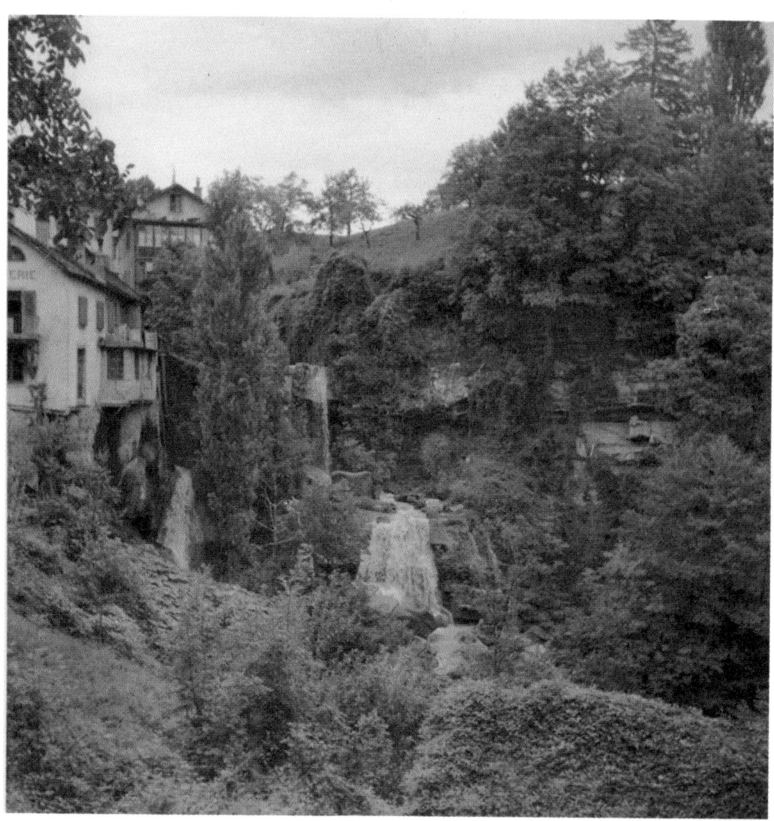

Fig. 39. Marcel Duchamp, *Swiss Landscape with Waterfall*, 1946. Gelatin silver print, 7⅛ × 6¾ in. (18.1 × 17.1 cm). Étant donnés Curatorial Records, Philadelphia Museum of Art, Library and Archives.

CREATION

Because of delays in getting his visa approved, Duchamp did not return to the United States until January of 1947, but we can be reasonably certain that as soon as he and Maria got together again, he began to work in earnest on the project he had in mind. As with his *Large Glass* years earlier, he had worked out most of the details in his head before he began its physical construction. He already had the sketch of Maria's foot, but now he needed to see her whole body exposed, so he again asked her to disrobe and pose for him. Once she was ready, he asked her to place her left leg onto a chair or some other support, so as to make her vulva and surrounding pubic hair clearly visible. The sketch he completed is naturalistically rendered, and I believe that, when he made it, he had already known that the figure would lie recumbent, but he needed a study that would not obscure from view through perspective or foreshortening any of the details of her anatomy he wished to render visible in his final vision of her fully exposed body (Fig. 40). The main feature of this drawing is pointed out by Duchamp's biographer, Calvin Tomkins, who described it as follows: "The view is

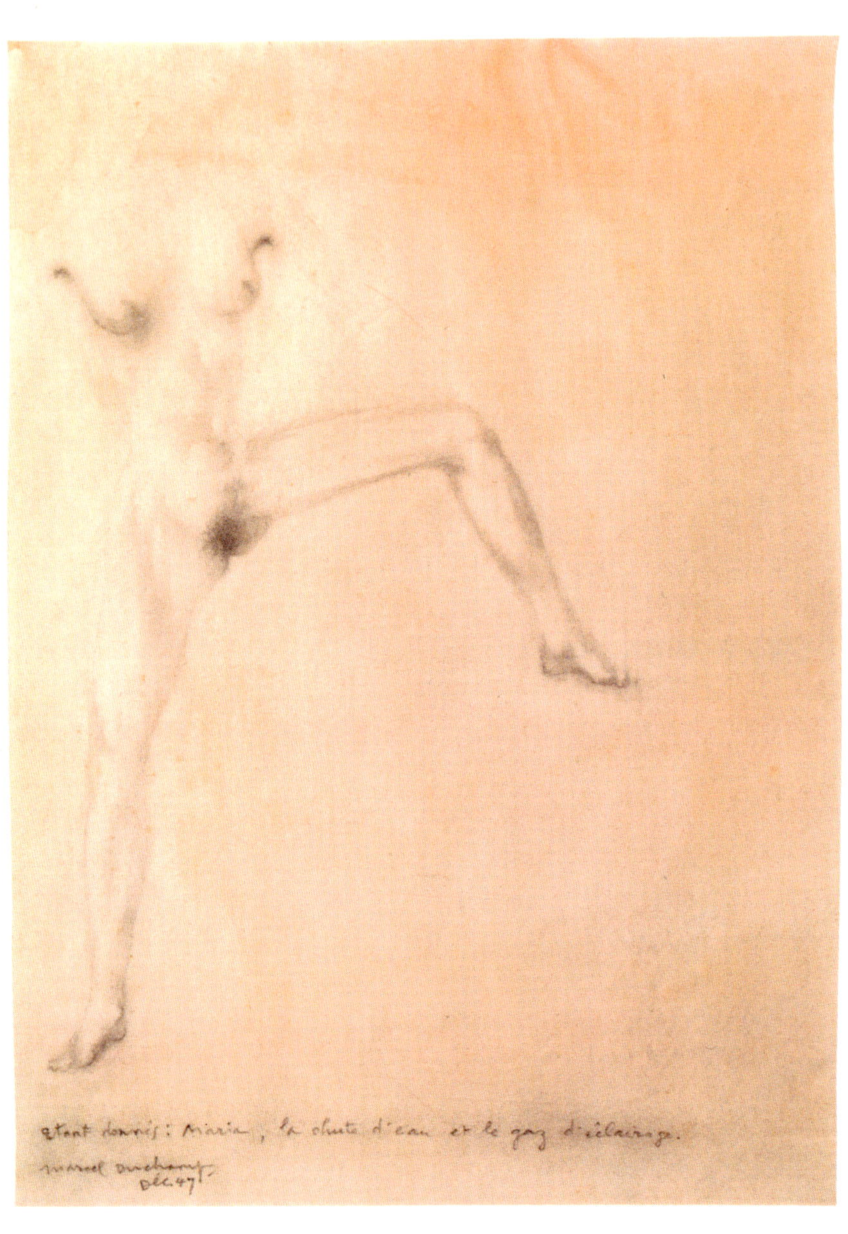

Fig. 40. Marcel Duchamp, *Étant donnés: Maria, la chute d'eau, et le gaz d'éclairage*, 1947. Pencil on paper, 15¾ × 11½ in. (40 × 29.1 cm). Moderna Museet, Stockholm; gift 1985, dedicated to Ulf Linde from Tomas Fischer.

frontal and its most prominent feature, rendered in slightly darker pencil lines than the rest of the composition, is her pubic bush."

If there is an immediate precedent to this drawing, it is not in Duchamp's work, but in Maria's. One could cite her earlier engraving of a nude woman lying on a spatial plane (Fig. 29), but a far more convincing comparison is with her *Je crus avoir longuement revé que j'étais libre* (Fig. 26), which features the close-focused view of a nude female figure whose upper body arches back and out of sight, but whose splayed legs and exposed crotch present themselves to the viewer openly and at eye level, without the slightest degree of modesty or shame (Fig. 26a). When Duchamp's drawing was completed, he signed and inscribed it at the base: *Étant donnés: Maria, la chute d'eau, et le gaz d'éclairage*, thereby identifying Maria as its subject and recording for posterity that she was the central focus of the last great work of art he was about to embark upon and work to complete for the next twenty years.

The next extant study for the *Étant donnés* that Duchamp completed is far more elaborate and detailed (Fig. 41). It shows a still standing figure, but the flesh of her body is here more clearly and precisely articulated, her breasts and abdomen rendered more photographic than graphic. This time, however, her outstretched body is nestled within a dense forest landscape, and a waterfall—the one Duchamp had photographed during his trip to Switzerland with Mary Reynolds (Fig. 39)— now rushes forth in a space below her outspread legs. Duchamp had these photographs printed and freely cut them up for use as collage elements within this composition; the vertical form in the center is a large poplar tree that covers a portion of the left leg of the figure, while still allowing her exposed crotch to be visible. This tree curiously resembles the projecting elements in Maria's *Je crus avoir longuement revé*—likely meant to represent foliage—which, depending on your point of view, obscure various elements of the sculpture. The rapport that exists between this sculpture and Duchamp's collage study is uncanny, proof not only of his attraction and dedication to the woman he loved, but evidence of how intently he internalized a visual memory of the sculpture she produced. In the work he was about to make with her complete approval and assistance, he found a means by which to capture her physical presence and retain it for himself, even if she were no longer a part of his life. Perhaps more than any other single factor, that realization—that he could physically possess her no matter how she felt about him (albeit in a surrogate fashion)—might have been the central motivating force behind the concept and construction of this last major work.

It would be easy to conclude that Maria harbored no serious affection for Marcel, but that could not be further from the truth. "She was very much in love with Duchamp," recalled Maria's daughter years later. It was her prior life commitments that prevented them from becoming the love-locked couple Duchamp might have desired, but she loved him just the same. It has been recently disclosed, for example, that in this period Maria kept a photograph of Duchamp on a charm bracelet that she wore, and, in another small compartment, she kept a lock of his hair (Fig. 42). Enrico Donati, the Italian-born Surrealist painter who befriended Duchamp and worked with him on several projects in

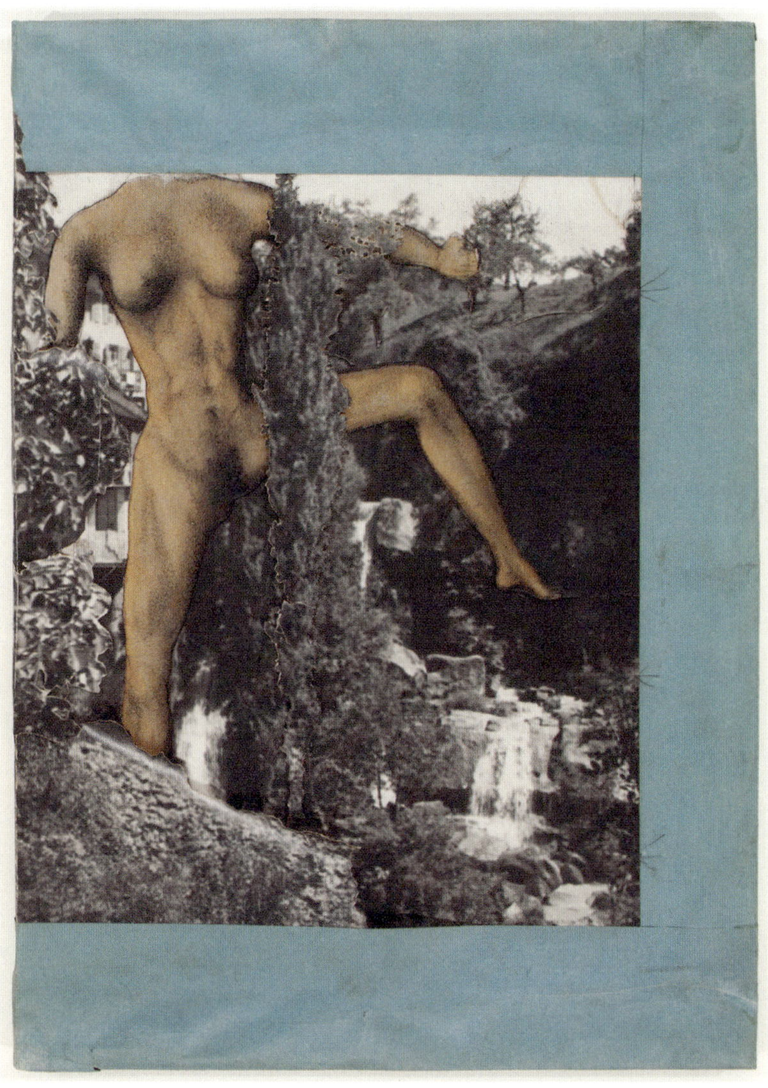

Fig. 41. Marcel Duchamp, *Untitled* (photocollage landscape study for *Étant donnés: 1° la chute d'eau, 2° le gaz d'éclairage*), c. 1947. Textured wax, pencil, and ink on tan paper and cut gelatin silver photographs mounted on board, 17 × 12¼ in. (43.2 × 31.1 cm). Bluff Collection.

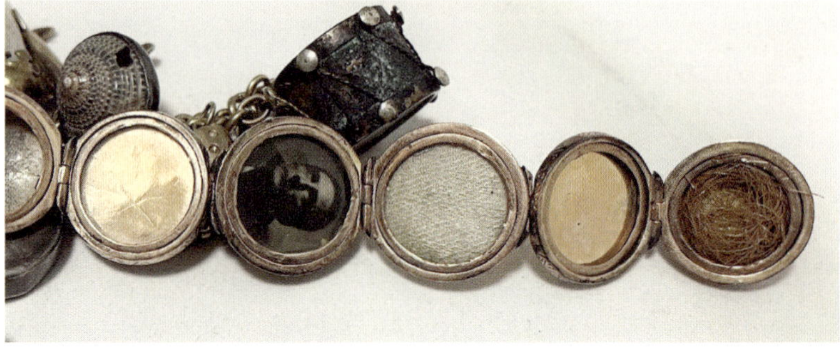

Fig. 42. Maria Martins's charm bracelet, c. 1945–47.
Collection Ignez Ceglia Simoes, Coconut Grove, Florida.

these years, later characterized their relationship as entirely symbiotic. "She [Maria] was madly in love with Duchamp," he recalled. "Everything Marcel said, she went 'ahhh' . . . you know. She clearly adored Marcel, and he was falling for her too, although he would never come out and say it." Donati never cared very much for Martins and struggled to understand what Marcel saw in her. "Maria was Brazilian, very beautiful, and full of life," he later explained. "Marcel had never met anyone like her, and she certainly had a deep impact on him. I think he was excited by their affair, but he also had an independent streak." According to Donati, Duchamp was attracted to the clandestine nature of their relationship: "He loved secrecy and being alone, so there was always going to be some unhappiness there." By 1948, Marcel and Maria were comfortable enough as a couple to be seen together with a number of close friends, as on an excursion they took one sunny summer afternoon in May with Donati and his wife Claire to the home of the artists Yves Tanguy and Kay Sage in Woodbury, Connecticut (Fig. 43). There they were joined by Frederick

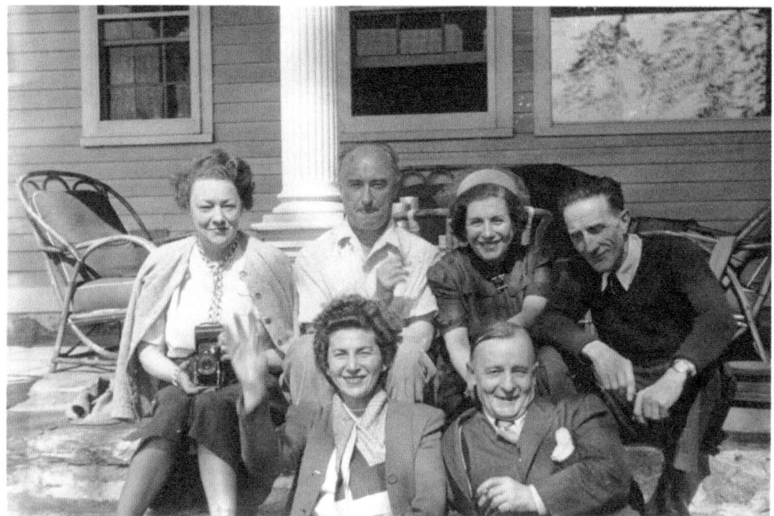

Fig. 43. Back row, from left to right: Kay Sage, Yves Tanguy, Maria Martins, Marcel Duchamp; front row: Claire Donati and Frederick Kiesler, Woodbury, Connecticut, May 23, 1948. Photo by Enrico Donati. Alexina and Marcel Duchamp Papers, Philadelphia Museum of Art, Library and Archives.

Kiesler, and, we can presume from the smiles on their faces, a good time was had by all. They played boules on the back lawn and Tanguy was especially impressed by Maria's sense of humor. "She is really charming," he reported in a letter to the French artist Marcel Jean in Paris a few months later, "and when she comes to see us we have good moments of genuine laughter." None of them, of course, knew about the true extent of Duchamp's involvement with Maria, especially not about the major work of art he was in the process of secretly constructing.

SURREALISM

When Duchamp was in Paris in 1946, he likely met with Breton to discuss the next great Surrealist exhibition that was scheduled for the Galerie Maeght the following year. Duchamp was entrusted with the design of the cover for the deluxe catalogue, and he came up with the idea of presenting the image of a woman's bare breast. For the regular trade edition of the publication, a photograph was taken of a woman's breast protruding through a hole cut in black velvet, which was reproduced on the cover of the catalogue. For the deluxe edition he planned to present impressions of an actual woman's breast, and he asked Maria if she would consider allowing him to cast hers. She willingly agreed. Several casts were taken (Fig. 44), but none proved satisfactory. Enrico Donati, who was helping Duchamp with this project, suggested using instead a woman's falsie, a fake breast that he had seen in a store for women's undergarments located near his studio. Duchamp liked the idea, so they ordered 999 examples from a supply shop in Brooklyn, but they arrived uncolored. After he had painted the first one, Donati turned to Duchamp and said in English, "Please touch." It was at that moment that the French title for

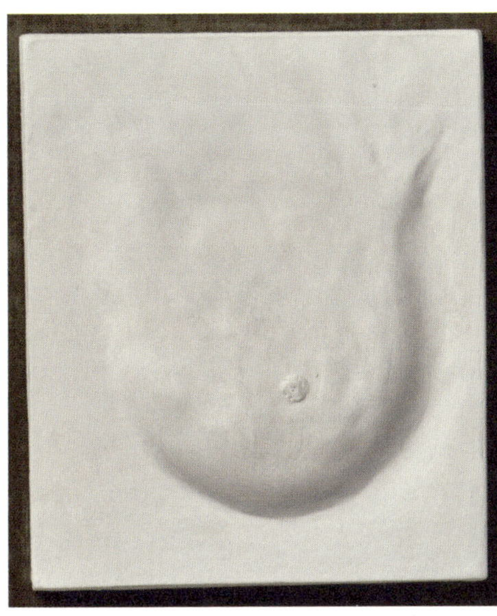

Fig. 44. Marcel Duchamp, study for *Prière de toucher* (Please Touch), 1947. Plaster, 8⅛ × 7⅛ in. (20.6 × 18.1 cm). Philadelphia Museum of Art; gift of Enrico Donati, 1997, 1997-33-1.

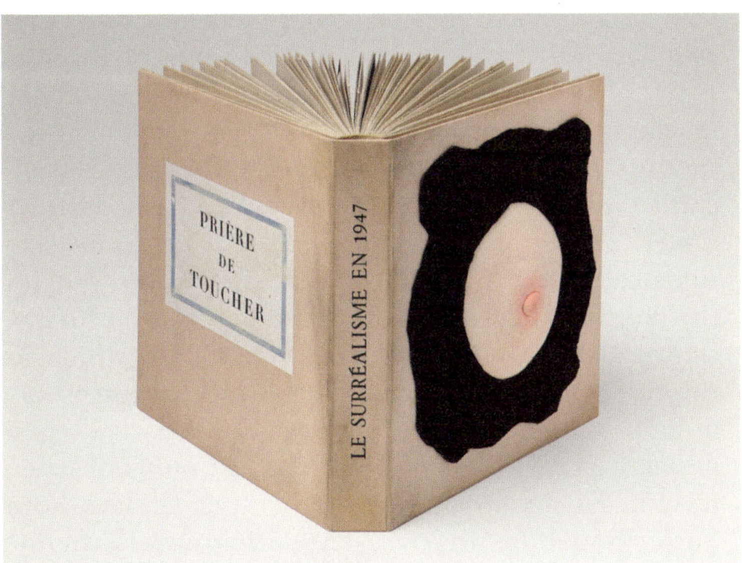

Fig. 45. Marcel Duchamp and Enrico Donati, *Prière de toucher* (Please Touch), 1947. Deluxe edition of the exhibition catalogue *for Le Surréalisme en 1947, Paris: Pierre à Feu/Maeght*, 1947. Book bound with collage of foam rubber, pigment, velvet, and cardboard adhered to removable cover, 9¼ × 8 in. (23.5 × 20.5 cm). Philadelphia Museum of Art; purchased with the Gertrude A. Memorial Fund, 1995-56-1.

the work was born: *Prière de toucher* was emblazoned on the back cover of every copy of the publication (both the regular and deluxe editions; Fig. 45). He and Donati spent weeks hand-painting the breasts and rubbing pigment into the nipples, a painstaking process that, according to Donati, drove them to the point of near insanity. "I never thought I would get tired of handling so many breasts," Donati told Duchamp, who immediately responded, "Maybe that's the whole idea."

Although it was likely Breton who determined the theme of the exhibition—which was dedicated to "modern myths"—it was Duchamp who was responsible for the exhibition's design and layout. He came up with the idea of a Hall of Superstitions, the Labyrinth, and the Rain Hall, "in which," as Marcel Jean later recalled, "he [Duchamp] recommended that a billiard table should be installed—one of the rare notes of deliberate humor in the exhibition." Since Duchamp was not in Paris at the time, he entrusted the installation to Frederick Kiesler, the Viennese architect in whose apartment in New York he had earlier rented a room. Kiesler followed Duchamp's instructions carefully, not only for the installation, but for the construction of a work he had conceived for the show called *La Rayon Verte* (The Green Ray), which, as the title suggests, re-creates the vision of a green ray of light that can be seen on a sea horizon at the first moment of a rising sun, or at the last moment when it sets. Duchamp also entrusted the Chilean-born Surrealist painter Roberto Matta—who with Katherine Dreier had written a book on *The Large Glass*—to construct and install his *The Juggler of Gravity*, a section of *The Large Glass* that was never completed,

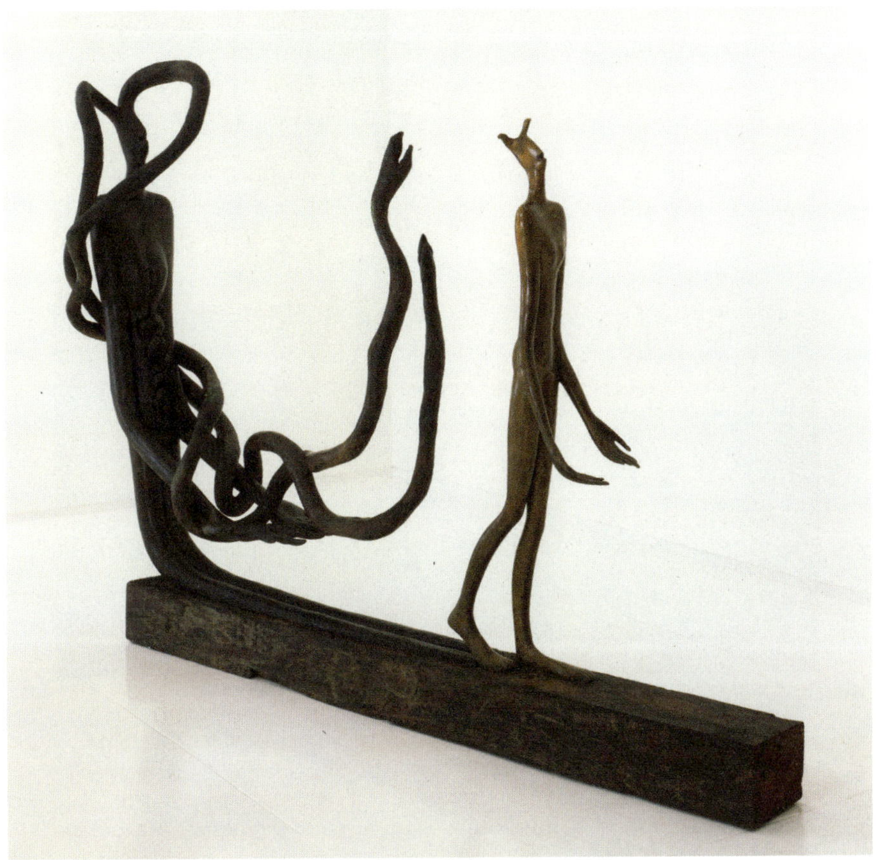

Fig. 46. Maria Martins, *The Road, The Shadow; Too Long, Too Narrow*, 1946. Bronze and wood, 56½ × 71¾ × 23⅜ in. (143.5 × 182.2 × 59.4 cm). Museum of Modern Art, New York; Brazil Fund.

but which was here re-created in the form of a three-dimensional tableau.

The Rain Room featured actual curtains of water cascading down into the room on artificial grass that drained from underneath wooden slats installed into

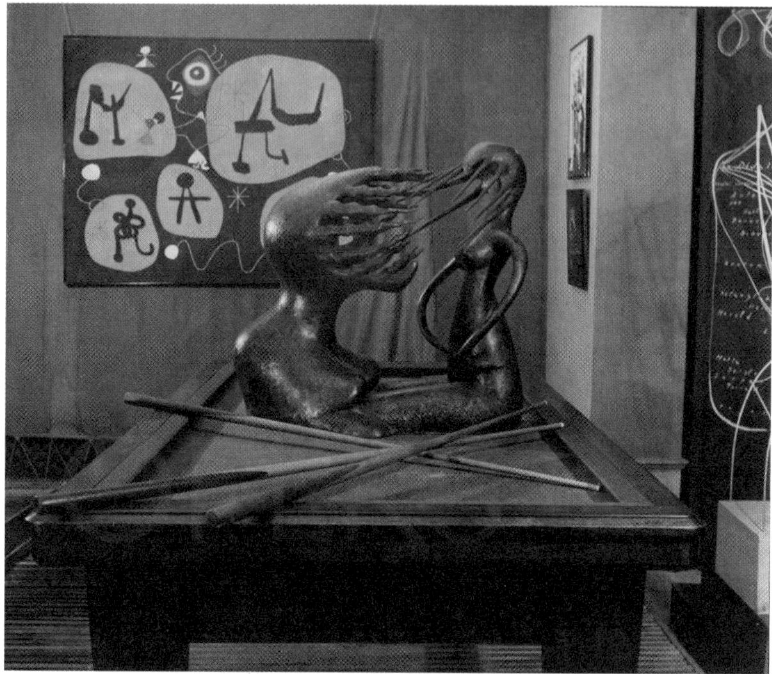

Fig. 47. *Rain Room, Exposition internationale du surréalisme*, Galerie Maeght, Paris, 1947. Installation photograph showing Maria Martins's sculpture *Impossible* on a billiard table with Joan Miró's *Femme entendent la musique* in the background. Vintage gelatin silver print on barite paper. Photograph by William Maywald. Austrian Frederick and Lillian Kiesler Private Foundation, Vienna.

the floor. It was in this room that Duchamp arranged for two of Maria's sculptures to be shown: a bronze cast of her *Impossible* and *The Road, The Shadow; Too Long, Too Narrow* (Fig. 46). *Impossible*—the version with curved arms—was positioned on a billiard table next to three overlapping pool cues (Fig. 47). On the other side of the room was positioned her other sculpture (Fig. 48), which features a nude female figure walking along a

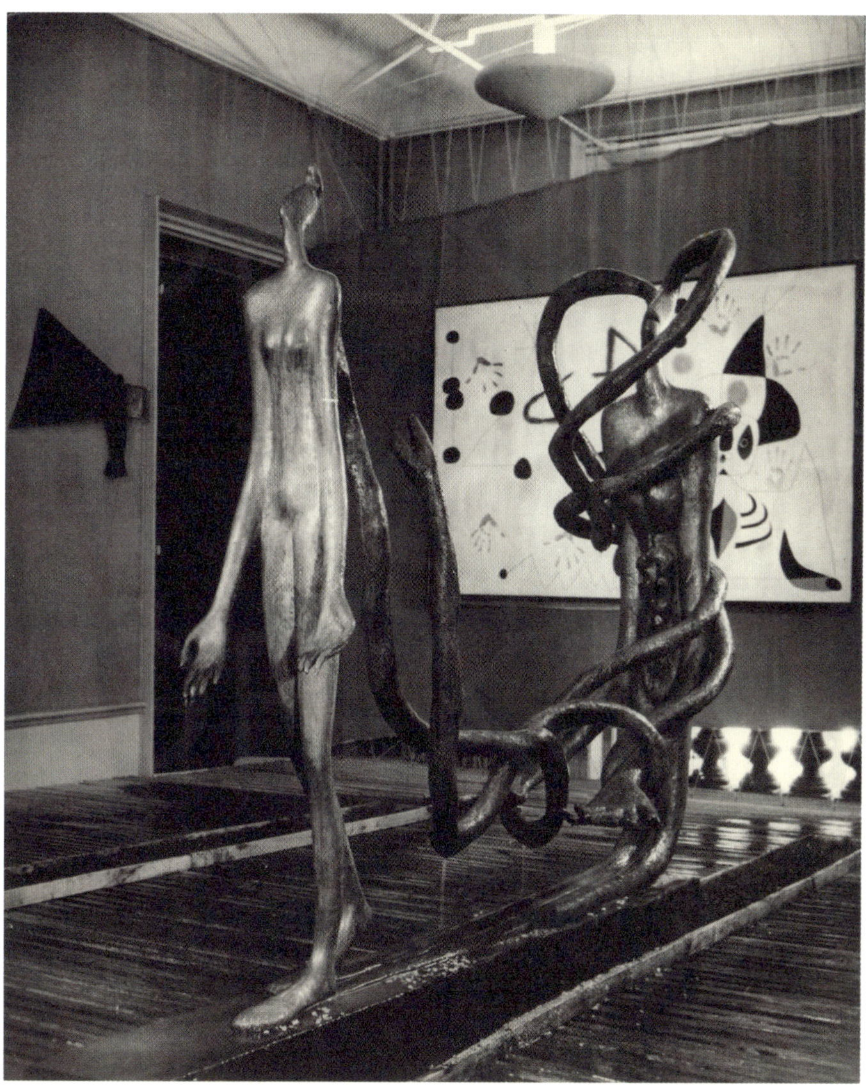

Fig. 48. *Rain Room, Exposition internationale du surréalisme*, Galerie Maeght, Paris, 1947. Installation photograph showing Maria Martins's sculpture *The Road, The Shadow; Too Long, Too Narrow* in the foreground and Joan Miró's *Woman in the Night* in the background. Vintage gelatin silver print on barite paper. Photograph by William Maywald. Austrian Frederick and Lillian Kiesler Private Foundation, Vienna.

rectangular beam, likely meant to represent the long and narrow road mentioned in the title. Her oversize hands are presented palms up, a gesture that suggests supplication, while a pair of small snakes appear to branch outward from the top of her animal-like head. Behind her emerges another form, clearly intended to represent her own cast shadow. A pair of snakes emerge from the shadow's head and gesture toward the back of the leading figure in a seemingly threatening manner, but she walks forward unaware of their existence. Shadows were a subject that had fascinated Duchamp since his early years in Paris, for they provided a convenient means by which to describe the fourth dimension. Maria, too, might be using the shadow for the same reasons, although her fourth dimension is not a mathematical world, but rather a mysterious domain in which serpents lurk behind the scenes acting as forces to control human destiny—much as they do in the various legends of the Amazon.

It is not known what visitors to the exhibition thought of these strange figures positioned in a room where rain was continuously falling, unless it was to remind them of the tropical environment from where the artist herself traced her origins and the myths that inspired her work. A few years earlier, Duchamp had told James Johnson Sweeney, a curator at the Museum of Modern Art who had planned to write a book on him, that the most important aspect of Martins's work was that it was "non-retinal," and that it had "acoustical" features. He probably had in mind sculptures like *Yara* (Fig. 6), which were meant to decorate a fountain, where the sound of water would have been an integral aspect of the work as it was being viewed by spectators.

He might also have wanted the sound of the rushing water in the Rain Room to enhance a viewer's experience of seeing work by an artist whose origins could be traced to the rainforest. Whatever the interpretation, there can be little doubt that Duchamp exerted his influence to have Maria's work included in this important exhibition, one that would serve to place her in the context of the most important European movement of the time: Surrealism.

The next major exhibition of Maria's work took place in the fall of 1947 at the Julien Levy Gallery, which by now had become known as the premier Surrealist showplace in New York. She had shown for years at the Valentine Gallery just down the street, but when it suddenly closed in 1947, she was without representation. We can be fairly certain that Duchamp also helped to orchestrate her new arrangement with Levy, who had been his close friend for years. The catalogue featured a long essay by André Breton (written in French and retained in that language for the American publication), wherein he observed that although Maria relies heavily on themes drawn from her youth in Brazil, she "owes nothing to the sculpture of the past or the present." He compared her most recent work to the sculpture of Brancusi, Arp, and Giacometti. A reviewer for the *New York Times* claimed the new works were a "more clearly plastic manifestation," by which he meant that the forms were less intricate and more sculptural than in her earlier work. He singled out *The Road . . .*, however, as "a subject painters rather than sculptors would ordinarily elect to depict," and he described *Impossible* as "two facing figures, massive, in white plaster, with festoons of spikes where their heads might logically be expected to appear." Finally, he felt that *Chansons en Suspens* (Songs in Suspense)—a work from 1943 that depicted a rooster playing a guitar—was "the most truly sculptural piece in the show." A more perceptive critic for *Artnews* may have hit upon the true essence of her work when he wrote: "No other sculptress is at once so much female and so little feminine."

The degree to which Maria was accepted by critics and her fellow artists as a bona fide Surrealist is difficult to determine, as she herself rejected the categorization. "Art exists only as an individual expression," she later explained. "It is an egregious error to consider that modern art necessarily obeys pre-established laws or a defined style (abstractionism, surrealism, figurativism [*sic*], etc.). The style in which a work of art is created is not important as long as it is impregnated with the spirit of its time and expressed in its own language, reflecting a powerful force that becomes tragic, less in terms of its appearance than its deep essence." There is no question that Maria felt honored to be included within the Surrealist circle, but like most artists, she felt that this type of classification made it difficult for others to see what she contributed that was uniquely an expression of her own sensibilities, independent of the stylistic qualities associated with the group.

Martins felt that human creativity offered a welcomed release from the trials and tribulations of everyday life, particularly in the aftermath of the war that had devastated Europe. She made this clear in a paper she prepared titled "Art, Liberation and Peace," a statement she arranged for Jacob Javits—a representative from the State of New York whom she had known from diplomatic circles in Washington, DC—to read into the

Congressional Record on June 18, 1947. "It was by the destruction of works of art . . . that Hitler began his nihilistic drive of conquest, domination and destruction," she wrote. "Art is liberation and construction; it is by art that we must rebuild this shattered world." She believed that art offered a universal panacea, a means by which to counter the destructive aspects of war. "Art is eternal not in its styles, not in its schools, not in its technique, not in its conceptions, nor in its subjects, but in its ideal, in its definition, in its aims, in its consequences. Art is the most solid basis of peace." It is unlikely that Duchamp would have shared such an optimistic point of view, for although he, too, valued creativity, he knew only too well that it was filtered through an art world based on criticism and judgment, an entrenched system that allowed certain artists to become famous while forgetting others. Later he would go so far as to say, "I don't believe in art," concluding, at least insofar as it pertained to his own work, that "art was a dream that's become unnecessary."

<h1 style="text-align:center">SEPARATION</h1>

About the time when Maria's show closed at the Julien Levy Gallery, she and her family moved to Paris, as her husband had been appointed Brazilian ambassador to France. For Duchamp, this must have been devastating news, as he cherished every moment he spent with her, but in her absence he would direct his energies to completing the project he had planned to immortalize her naked body in a landscape. The advantage to posterity of their separation is that they communicated through writing, and Duchamp's letters to Maria were preserved and survive (whereas hers to him were destroyed by Duchamp himself, likely shortly after he had responded to them). If these missives—most of which are undated—are read in the order in which they are believed to have been written, the process Duchamp undertook in the making of the figure in this environmental tableau can be partially reconstructed. We are at the same time provided with an often-painful account of Duchamp's inability to give up on his romantic quest for Maria, who remained unattainable and was now living some three thousand miles away in, of all places, his former hometown. Duchamp might even have given some thought to joining her, but he knew that he would have to live with the frustration of only meeting with her in secrecy, an arrangement that, by then, was likely taking its toll on the emotional well-being of both lovers.

In the summer of 1948, while Maria was in Paris, Duchamp wrote to let her know that Mary Reynolds was back in New York. "Nothing will change our love," he reassures her. "Nothing has happened nor will happen." But a week later, having returned from a chess tournament in Endicott, New York, he wrote again, telling her that "these 8 days in the country have done me a wealth of good. I had a lot of free time between games and I thought about us a good deal. How simple life is when there is only the inner self to think about. So I took a trip inside your inner self, and I found what I had thought would be there, having guessed by external contact only—I found 'things' that have no name in the most poetical language. We must live by these 'things' and by these 'things' alone. The rest, mere physical survival, must be reduced to the minimum." He concludes the letter by saying, "I am returning tomorrow and will go back to my dry skin under its steel rods," adding, "Only you can understand this sentence." He signed the letter, as he had the previous three sent to her, with a single word: *Amour.*

The "dry skin under its steel rods" can only refer to his work on constructing the figure in the *Étant donnés*, for at the time he was still experimenting with a method to secure the figure's skin to its support, the steel rods being used as weights to keep the skin in place. He is right in saying that only Maria could understand what he is writing about, because at the time, not another single person knew about the project he was working on with her. He was then likely in the process of completing a preliminary study of the figure with graphite and leather laid over plaster, which he surrounded with irregular amorphic shapes covered in velvet (Fig. 49). Once it was completed, he gave it as a gift to Maria, inscribing it *Cette dame appartient à Maria Martins / avec toutes mes affections / Marcel Duchamp 1948–49* ("This lady is owned by Maria Martins / with all my affection / Marcel Duchamp 1948–49"), which he followed with fairly elaborate instructions on its lighting and care. He was especially concerned that the pencil marks on the leather be preserved: "In case of restoration or reframing," he wrote, "avoid touching the woman since her skin is speckled in the shadows with lead pencil—this lead pencil is not fixed and it could not be fixed (even a light fixative washes away and makes the lead pencil disappear)." These written instructions were not likely meant solely for Maria, as Duchamp could have conveyed them to her orally, but rather for those who would be entrusted to care for this object in the future. He knew that this work—and, for that matter, any other works he made—would survive his lifetime and even Maria's (which, of course, is precisely what occurred). But what, it is reasonable to wonder, did he think Maria would do with this work after he gave it to her? Did he expect her to bring it home and hang it on her wall, where her husband and others would clearly inquire as to exactly whose naked body it represented, or did he instruct her to keep it out of view for an indefinite period of time? We may never know what arrangement they had, but we do know that Maria hung it in her bedroom after her husband's death, and she did not allow it to be shown publicly until long after

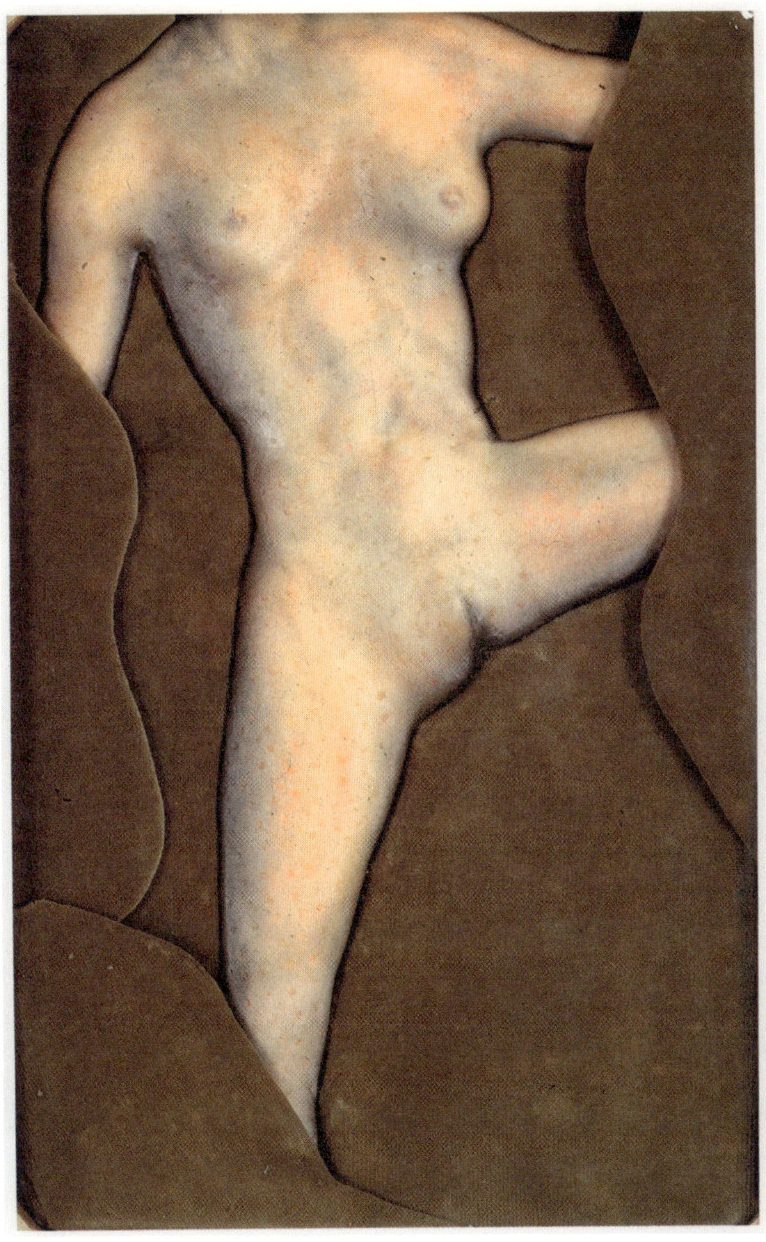

Fig. 49. Marcel Duchamp, *Study for Étant donnés*, c. 1946–48. Pigment and graphite on leather-covered plaster with velvet, 19¾ × 12¼ in. (50.2 × 31.1 cm). Moderna Museet, Stockholm; gift 1985, dedicated to Ulf Linde from Tomas Fischer.

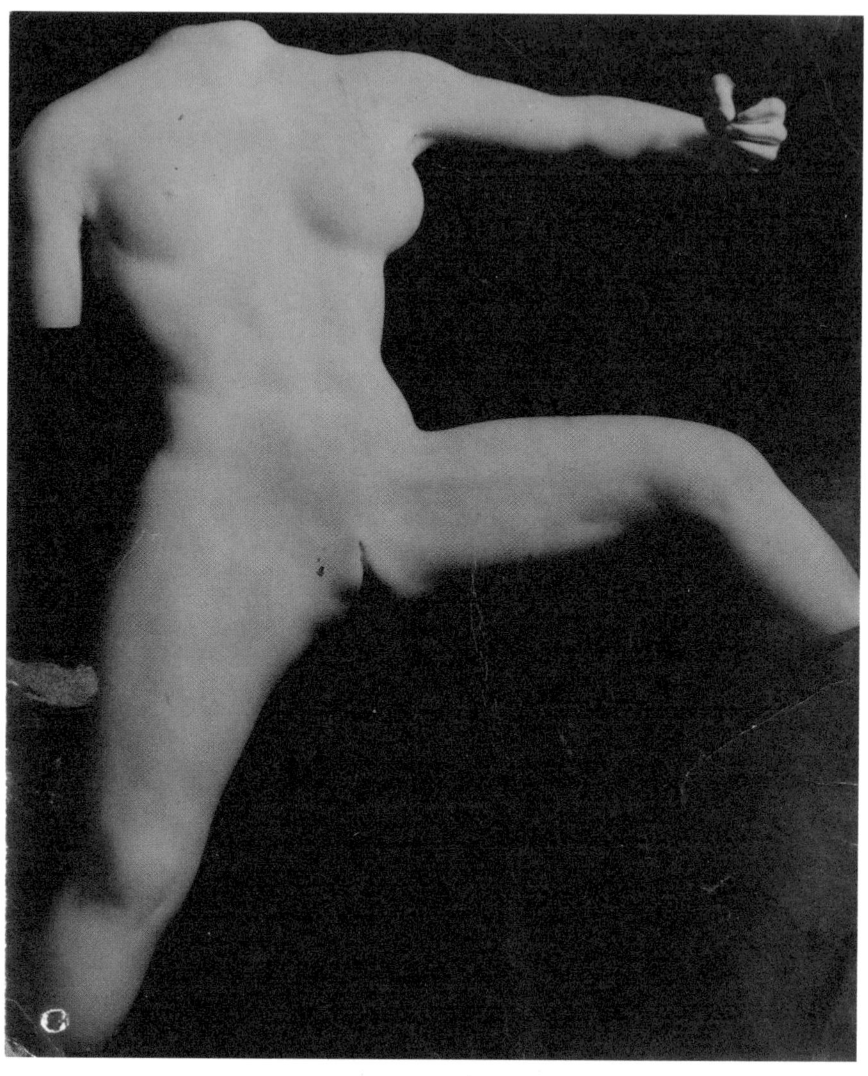

Fig. 50. Marcel Duchamp, figure study for *Étant donnés*, c. 1949.
Photograph, 9¼ × 7½ in. (23.5 × 19 cm). San Francisco
Museum of Modern Art; gift of the Nora and Norman Stone Collection.

her affair with Duchamp was over (although as we shall see, she did send it to an exhibition in 1966, two years before his death).

In one of the many letters that Duchamp sent to Maria in Paris updating her on the progress he was making in rendering the figure, he enclosed a black-and-white photograph of a plaster sculpture he had made of her body (Fig. 50). "I would like you to keep for yourself this unique example of direct sculpture," he wrote, "for as the photo already shows, it no longer has anything to do with the plasteline model I had cast less than six months ago." In examining this photograph, ones sees that the hair in the figure's pubic area and armpits has been removed, likely for the purpose of facilitating the casting process. When a cast is made of the human body, the skin must be covered with some sort of gelatinous substance like petroleum jelly, or the plaster or wax will adhere to the surface of the skin and make it difficult to remove, particularly when attempting to take an impression of human hair. It is far easier for the hair to be removed before beginning the casting process, so it is likely that Duchamp asked Maria to shave beforehand, or, for all we know, he might have shaved her himself. We know that Duchamp seems to have had an aversion to body hair. Some twenty-five years earlier, he and Man Ray had made a film of them shaving the pubic hair from the body of the eccentric German model Baroness Elsa von Freytag-Loringhoven, and when he married his first wife, Duchamp asked her to shave these areas of her body. He didn't even like hair on any part of his own body, except, of course, what was on his head. "His body was permanently shorn of all unwanted hair," his first wife recalled.

"He had an almost pathological horror of anything that resembled hair." We do not know if Duchamp intended to replace the hair that was removed on the final rendition of this work, as some have suggested; it is doubtful that he would have done so, since he had already left the figure fully denuded in the preliminary study he gave to Maria (Fig. 49).

Looking at this photograph carefully, we will notice that the figure's upraised left arm ends in a hand that seems to be holding a pole or some other cylindrical object that she presents to the viewer. A detailed drawing that Duchamp made of this hand reveals exactly what it was intended to hold: a mirror that, for all intents and purposes, would have been designed to reflect back at the viewer (Fig. 51). Later he would replace this element with a gas lantern, but for the time being, it looks like he planned to use a mirror. Some would likely disagree with this assumption, as Duchamp had already determined that the title of this work would be *Given: The Waterfall, the Illuminating Gas*, and since we know that he had intended to represent the waterfall somewhere in the background behind the figure, then, we could rightly ask, where had he planned to represent the illuminating gas? One possible answer is that he might have intended to depict it in some other form, either as a gas lantern mounted elsewhere in the environment, or simply as a light coming from a source not visible to the viewer, but its reflection (by means of the mirror), very much in evidence. The reason a mirror makes so much sense in this context is because—as Duchamp wrote in the same note for *The Large Glass* that he gave to Maria a few years earlier (Fig. 33)—the Bachelors respond to all question of love with a mirror

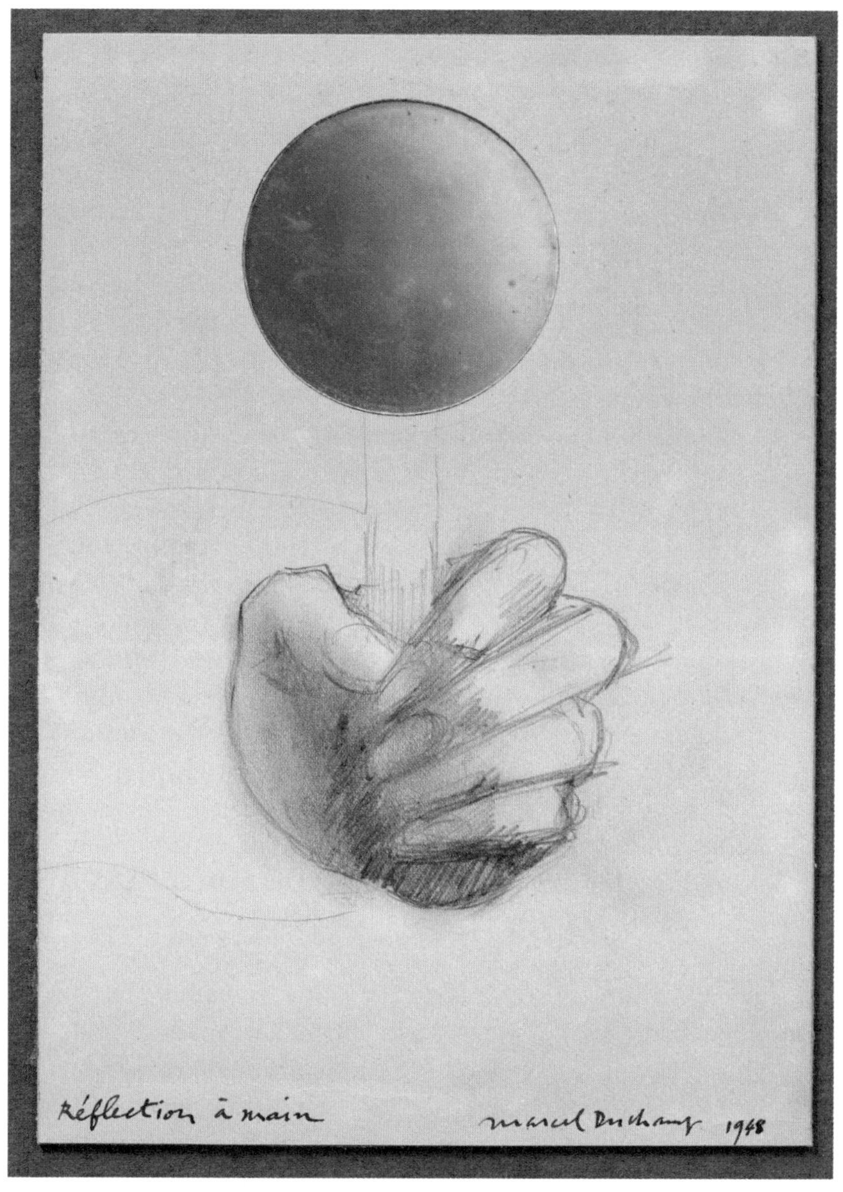

Fig. 51. Marcel Duchamp, *Réflection à main*, 1948. Pencil
on paper, mirror, and ink inscription, mounted under
plexiglass into the lid of a deluxe *Boîte-en-valise*, no. XVII/
XX, 9¼ × 6½ in. (23.5 × 16.5 cm). Private collection, Paris.
Photograph © 2024 Christie's Images Limited.

that reflects "back to them their own complexity, deluding them fairly onanistically."

In many of his letters to Maria, Duchamp expressed his frustration about their living situation, since he found their separation from each other for such long periods excruciating. In a letter that he sent from San Francisco—where he had gone in the spring of 1949 to participate in a roundtable on modern art—he told her "I realize just how much both of us are imprisoned by a gang of so called 'friends' who are not out to do us any wrong as such but who simply want to keep us in a cage." He openly wonders how the situation can ever be resolved. "I spend a lot of time thinking of a way to escape from the cage. Nor must we let ourselves be trapped by our 'environment.'" He then reminds her of a solution that they had already agreed upon. "As we have always said, the way out is your sculpture and my woman with the open pussy." Put another way, they should both find refuge in their work, for only there could they avoid being entrapped by the restrictions that—through no fault of their own—were imposed on their lives. Throughout their correspondence, Duchamp refers to the mannequin he is working on as "ours," implying that it exists as a product of their artistic collaboration. Perhaps fearing that his letters might be discovered, he refers to the work in a coded language, several times calling it *N.D. des désirs* or *Notre Dame des désirs* (Our Lady of Desires), an intentionally sacrilegious way of referring to the sculpture that only Maria would have understood. In his letters, Duchamp tried to put an optimistic spin on the impracticality and impossibility of their relationship, but over time, he became increasingly disheartened. "What is the situation now?" he asked in a letter also written in the spring of 1949. "At heart, my little one, I am profoundly sad, for I can see all our days passing rapidly and fading away one by one without any of our dreams coming true. Is it because we lack courage? Why should we give in when nothing is really an obstacle? I love you but I would like to love you better."

While in Paris, Maria did continue to work feverishly on her art. She first took a studio in the Villa d'Alesia, lent to her by the Brazilian painter Cicero Dias and located right across the street from Brancusi's studio on the Impasse Ronsin. Maria had known the Romanian sculptor since 1938, introduced to him while she was living in Belgium by the art dealer Joseph Brummer (who showed Brancusi in his New York gallery). "The simplicity of forms had achieved total purity," she would say of Brancusi's sculpture, "keeping, however, the visible palpitation of a profound inner life that made them illuminate the entire environment." Brancusi and Maria got along very well, sharing many of the Romanian sculptor's famous home-cooked peasant meals. After only a few months in this location, she moved to a studio on the rue de l'Université, closer to the Drouin Gallery, where we can imagine she worked tirelessly to complete a series of new sculptures for her forthcoming show there, which was planned for the fall of 1948. It was during this time in Paris that she entered into correspondence with Francisco Matarazzo Sobrinho, president of the Museum of Modern Art in São Paulo, for he had asked her to help with the organization of the first Biennale in Brazil. Maria put Matarazzo in contact with Duchamp in New York, who, with the help of various dealers (he mentions specifically Sidney

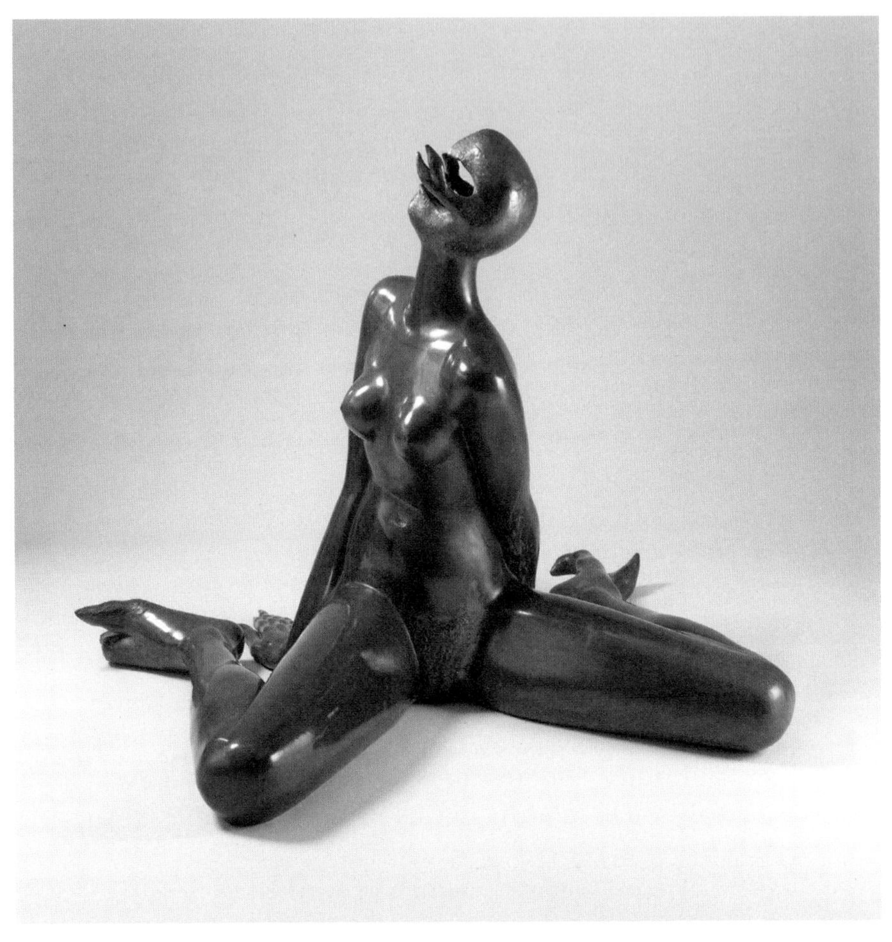

Fig. 52. Maria Martins, *Huitième Voile* (Eighth Veil), 1948.
Polished bronze cast, 1949, 41 × 45 × 37 in. (104 × 114 × 94 cm).
Collection Geneviève Boghici, Rio de Janeiro.

Janis and Leo Castelli), promised to arrange for the shipment of forty paintings to Brazil. For her part, Maria arranged for works to be sent from Paris, and agreed to show her sculpture in part of the exhibition reserved for Brazilian art.

Maria's show at the Drouin Gallery contained many new large-scale sculptures, including a bronze sculpture called *However* and another called *The Woman Who Has Lost Her Shadow*, each more than nine and a half feet tall. Both sculptures represent the bodies of naked women with distorted heads, one with legs enwrapped by a large serpent, and the other the female figure that appeared at the forefront of her earlier sculpture *The Road, The Shadow; Too Long, Too Narrow* (Fig. 46), but here she appears alone, having lost, as the title indicates, her shadow. The show was accompanied by a book called *Les Statues Magiques* containing texts by André Breton (the same one he had written for the Julien Levy Gallery) and the French critic Michel Tapié, who wrote of Maria: "Your statues are a good illustration of the apparent contradictions which make Magic (life Life) seem to run on Paradoxical Terror." The book reproduces work created by Maria throughout her career, as well as several sculptures made specially for this exhibition, such as her monumental *The Eighth Veil*, reproduced in the publication as a plaster sculpture, as the bronze would only be cast in the following year (Fig. 52). Maria must have sent a copy of this publication to Duchamp, for he singled out this sculpture in particular. "I like the 8th Veil a great deal," he wrote, "and its head, though I can't see it clearly even with a magnifying glass." He asks her to send other photos if she can, but his interest in making out the head in this sculpture is intriguing, for there is an unmistakable rapport between it and the nude female figure he was working on at the time, which, of course, would never be given a head with features that could be identified by the viewer.

Maria's *Eighth Veil* is a visually arresting image. It consists of a nude female figure—deftly articulated and based on the body of her daughter, who was studying to become a professional dancer—seated on a flat horizontal surface with her legs spread wide apart, her pubic hair carefully and clearly articulated for all to see. Her hands and feet are rendered as grotesque, monstrous appendages that look more animal than human. The head is little more than a spherical void. In the plaster, a pair of snakes issue from the woman's cheek, but in the bronze they are reduced to menacing, claw-like projections. The work closely resembles Maria's earlier depiction of Salome (1939), but in addition to the changes made to the head and hands, *Eighth Veil* is conspicuously missing the veil that was used to cover the leg of the earlier figure; if Salome was known for her Dance of the Seven Veils, then Maria's allusion to an "eighth veil" must refer to the tragic result of her lascivious dance: the removal of St. John the Baptist's head. It is possible that in her creation of this sculpture, Maria was making the image of a female figure that presented to the viewing public her entirely naked anatomy—what is today called full-frontal nudity—while at the same time, subtly defying Duchamp's aversion to pubic hair.

ACQUIESCENCE

In early November of 1949, Carlo Martins retired from diplomatic life and moved from Paris to Brazil. He immediately returned to Rio de Janeiro, but Maria stopped for a short visit in New York, ostensibly with the mission of trying to interest young American artists and writers in visiting her native country, but also probably to clean out and pack up her apartment. She seized the opportunity to see Duchamp once again and gave several interviews to the press. "We do not need a Marshall Plan for Brazil," she told a journalist, "but we would like a greater sharing of ideas and art with our neighbors." When she was asked about her own work, she explained that it was of the same type that she had done while living in the United States. "After all," she said, "I am of the school of New York." Maria would live out the remaining years of her life in Brazil, where at first she was greeted with considerable hostility by critics who regarded her an outsider, too long removed from the country of her birth to be considered a part of its artistic heritage. Besides, her Surrealist work was considered out of sync with the prevalent artistic style in Brazil at the time, Geometric Abstraction. In the catalogue for the retrospective exhibition of her work that was mounted at the Museum of Modern Art in São Paulo in 1950, as if in anticipation of her detractors, she published an excerpt from Duchamp's comments in the Western Round Table on Modern Art, which had taken place only a year earlier in San Francisco. "Criticism against modern art is the natural consequence of the freedom given the artist to express his individualistic view," he said. "Moreover, I consider the barometer of opposition a healthy indication of the depth of individual expression. The more hostile the criticism, the more encouraged the artist should be." Duchamp's presence was also felt in the design of the exhibition's checklist: the title of each of the thirty-six sculptures included in the exhibition was set in a completely different type, a unique style of typography he pioneered and used in several earlier publications.

With Maria now living so far away from him in Brazil, Duchamp was finally beginning to give up on his dream of their life together. "I feel totally lost now that we are completely cut off from each other," he wrote in the spring of 1950. "This isolation hurts." Later in the same letter he writes, "I can't even say 'write' anymore. This situation is driving me to despair." Nearly a year later he wrote, "You are condemned and damned to suffer unnecessarily, and that is the tragedy of your situation. The net you are caught in is made of such thick rope that not even a razor blade could cut you free. I suffer, my little one, more than you, because I could save myself if I were in your position but can do nothing except talk to you through holes in the net." A few months later he wrote, "There is no ersatz love. It does not exist. And by not making love we feel disgust and there is no way out. Every work is a sexual stimulant, instead of turning our attention away from the physiological." Consider these excerpts from letters all written in the fall of 1951, which increasingly reveal that he is slowly coming to accept the end of their affair: "I think of you, of us, and I can't help but feel great sorrow, which I try to chase away by thinking of our brief good times" (October 17); "I have come to accept the situation as it is and no longer seek to find some miracle solution" (October 25); "What has become of us, apart from, forever far apart. I can't help constantly thinking of the stupid nonsense that keeps us separated. Love is not made of feats of endurance—and I find it terrifying to think that I can almost count on my fingers the number of times I will see you again in the whole of the rest of my life" (November 9). It was probably with one of these letters that Duchamp included a piece of paper from a notepad printed with the words "Please Do Not Throw This on Floor" (Fig. 53). On this sheet he touchingly drew a heart in ink that he colored with red crayon, writing the words below: "That is for Maria." He unquestionably understood their relationship as a true *affaire de coeur*.

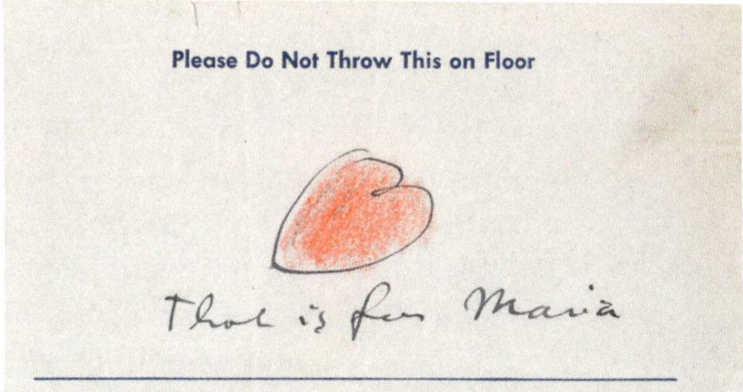

Fig. 53. Marcel Duchamp, *That is for Maria (Please Do Not Throw This on Floor)*, c. 1951. Ink and crayon on printed notepaper, 3 × 5½ in. (7.6 × 14 cm). Marcel Duchamp Association, Paris.

TIMING

uchamp's separation from Maria could not have occurred at a more opportune moment in his life, for it
was precisely then—in the fall of 1951—that he started
dating Alexina Sattler Matisse, known to friends as
"Teeny," the former wife of the art dealer Pierre Matisse
(son of Henri). He first met her in 1923 and had seen
her often in social settings over the years. Duchamp
found her to be not only a lovely woman, but also an
instinctively gifted chess player. Although they would
never play against each other (the game is too compet-
itive and combative), they reviewed the scores of prior
games, watched others play at chess clubs, and later
even attended tournaments together. This was a person with whom he could share his passion. She was not
only exceptionally compatible and agreeable to be with,
but as her prowess at the game of chess convincingly
demonstrated, was a profoundly intelligent person, a
quality that Duchamp was unquestionably drawn to
and which he admired. It would not have been long
before he told her about the project he had been working on with Maria, likely bringing her to his studio
and showing her the naked body to which he had been

attempting to give form with painstaking similitude. How she initially reacted is difficult to say, for although she helped him with the project in any way she could— even allowing for her arm and hand to be cast holding a lantern (after he had switched from his earlier idea of having the figure hold a mirror)—in the years after Duchamp's death she revealed to friends that she really didn't like the work. Today it is difficult to know if her objections were based on seeing such a realistic portrayal of a woman's body placed in such a compromising position—her genitals openly exposed for everyone to see—or whether her distaste for the work was more personal, a jealousy for the deep love Duchamp harbored for another woman, even if that relationship took place years earlier and had ceased. What we do know is that she did not want more attention paid to the work than was absolutely necessary.

Not long after showing this work to Teeny, Duchamp became heavily involved in installing the collection of Louise and Walter Arensberg in the galleries of the Philadelphia Museum of Art. Aside from a remarkably comprehensive collection of modern art, the Arensbergs had amassed the largest single collection of his work— more than thirty-eight items, including two versions of his *Nude Descending a Staircase*—all of which they left to the museum. In 1952, Duchamp also arranged for *The Large Glass* (Fig. 19), which was then still owned by Katherine S. Dreier, to be given to the museum as well. Duchamp spent a considerable amount of time at the museum installing these works, particularly his *Large Glass*, which was set between two vertical aluminum poles that went from the floor to the ceiling in one of the main galleries (Fig. 54). Duchamp instructed that a

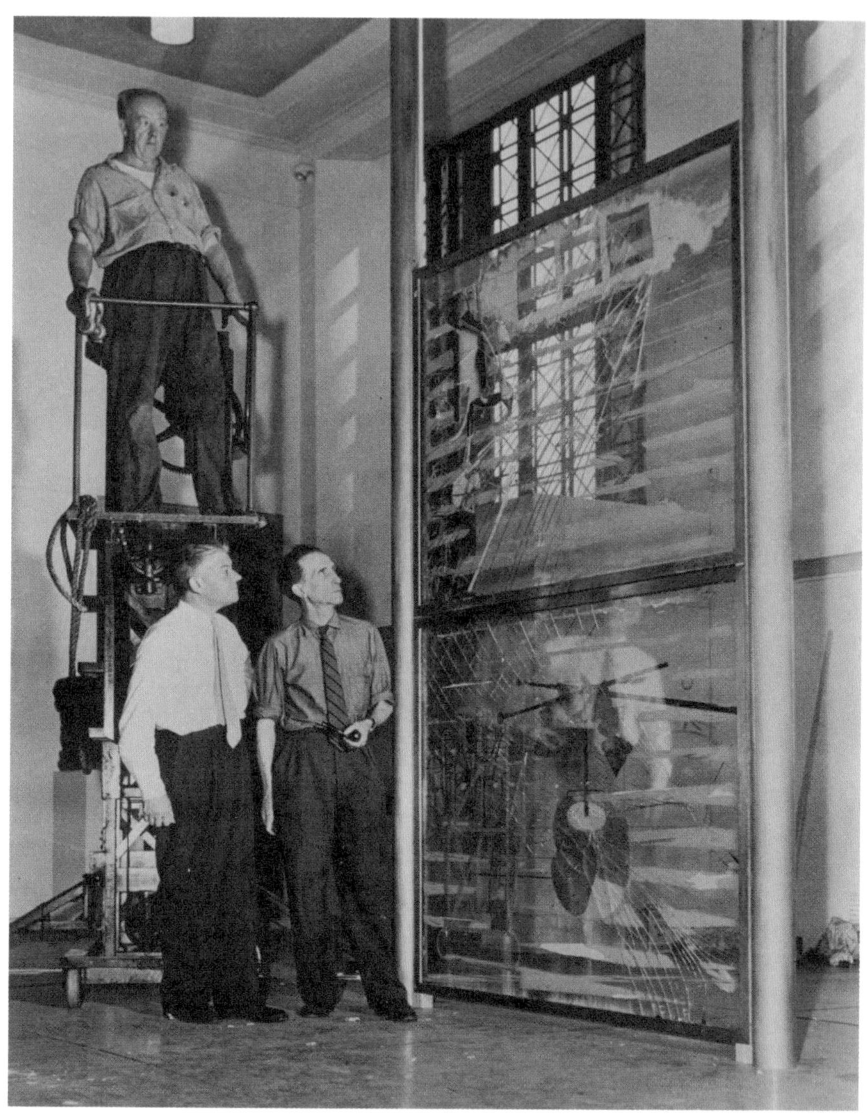

Fig. 54. Marcel Duchamp installing *The Large Glass*
at the Philadelphia Museum of Art, July 19, 1954.
Marcel Duchamp Exhibition Records, Philadelphia
Museum of Art, Library and Archives.

door be opened in the wall behind *The Large Glass* that led to a balcony, where, across the terrace and beyond the fountain, could be seen Maria's *Yara* (Fig. 6), which had been on display in that spot since 1942. Duchamp seems to have not told anyone at the museum, and, insofar as we know, not even Teeny (whom he married in 1954), why this door needed to be there, other than to say that he wanted the fountain and a bit of nature to be seen through *The Large Glass*. The relationship between *The Large Glass* and Maria's *Yara* was only noticed for the first time in 1992, more than twenty-four years after Duchamp's death, by a German art historian. When installing this work in 1954, however, he had planned that another major work of his would eventually be added to this ensemble, one that would unify Maria's *Yara* with not only *The Large Glass*, but with the large-scale environmental construction that he was still working to complete back in his New York studio.

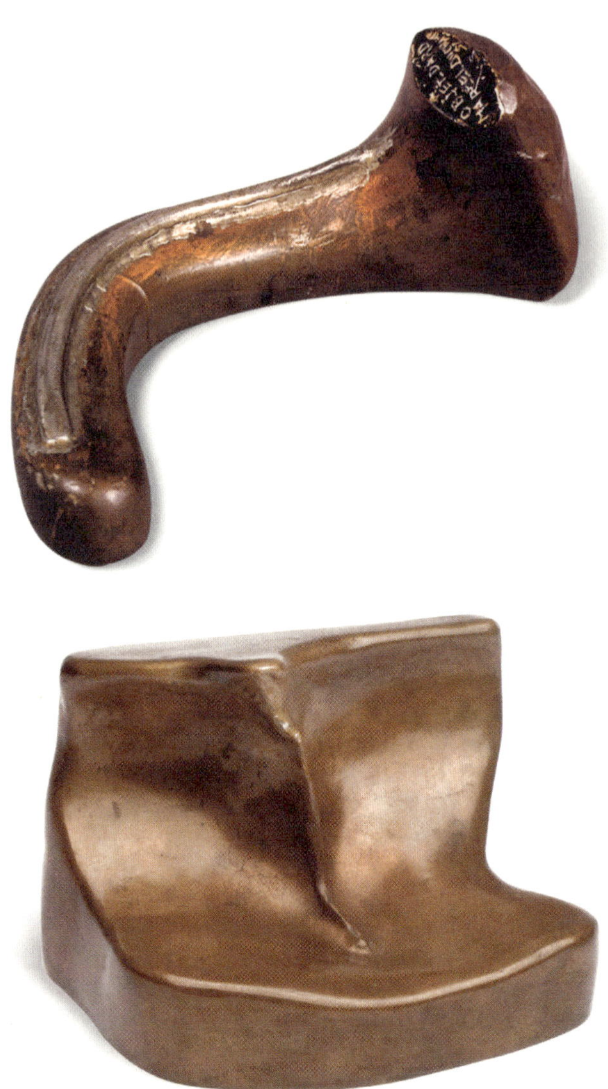

Fig. 55. Marcel Duchamp, *Objet-Dard* (Dart Object), 1951.
Copper-electroplated plaster cast with inlaid lead rib,
3 × 8 × 2⅔ in. (7.5 × 20.2 × 6 cm). Private Collection.

Fig. 56. Marcel Duchamp, *Feuille de vigne femelle* (Female Fig Leaf),
1950. 1951 cast of 1950 copper-electroplated plaster original
painted plaster cast, 3½ × 5¾ × 5 in. (8.9 × 14.6 × 12.7 cm).
Philadelphia Museum of Art; gift of Mme Marcel Duchamp.

KEEPING A SECRET

Despite the fact that he told no one else about the *Étant donnés* project and would try to keep it a secret until his death, over the years Duchamp released works of art that were related to it, although virtually no one at the time knew exactly what to make of them. In December of 1953, for example, he participated in a two-person show with Francis Picabia at the Rose Fried Gallery in New York, where he exhibited examples of earlier work—a *Green Box*, a *Boîte-en-valise*—but also two curious objects that would have come as a surprise to anyone familiar with his work: *Objet-Dard* (Fig. 55) and *Feuille de Vigne Femelle* (Fig. 56), the first identified in the catalogue as simply a sculpture, the second a plaster cast, both made in 1951. Visitors to the exhibition would not have expected to see new work like this by the artist, because he was thought to have abandoned active artistic production years earlier, preferring instead to play chess and issue occasional editions that were variations on earlier work (essentially, the other works by him shown in this same exhibition). Besides, these objects took on the appearance of traditional sculpture, a medium that—like painting—was assumed to have been superseded by Duchamp's introduction of the ready-made some forty years earlier.

So exactly what were these strange artifacts? *Objet-Dard* translates as "Dart Object," but how is this strangely shaped artifact the object of a dart, or could it be the dart itself? The object was made from a bent cylindrical shape that, upon first examination, struck viewers as somewhat phallic, but, because of its curving profile, possibly a penis rendered in a flaccid state. The title is a homophone for *object d'art*, but it would translate literally as "dart object." Those who spoke French well would have known that the term *dard* is slang for penis, reinforcing its phallic appearance. The other object, *Feuille de Vigne Femelle* translates as "Female Fig Leaf," and there could be no question that this term also related to an equally intimate body part, but this time derived from the female anatomy. Moreover, since this object was identified as a plaster cast, one could only imagine that it was an impression made directly from a woman's pubis, although this sort of a specific observation would have been considered inappropriate to express publicly. Critics of the exhibition were equally bewildered. *The New York Times* called them "bizarre artifacts," while a reviewer for *Arts & Architecture* described the *Objet-Dard* as "bronze, phallic [and] male," and the *Female Fig Leaf* as "plaster, triangular [and] *très femelle*." A reviewer for *Art Digest* said they "both reveal a command of sculptural design as well as a characteristic stab of malice." Whereas most visitors to the exhibition would have been able to figure out that these objects were intended to convey some sort of erotic meaning (particularly in light of their provocative titles), virtually no one—not even those familiar with Duchamp's earlier artistic production—would have been able to identify their specific origin or meaning in his work.

Man Ray—Duchamp's close friend and artistic collaborator during the years they spent together in New York and Paris—is among the few who may have known more about these objects than anyone else at the time (save the artist himself), for he was entrusted by Duchamp to replicate one of them. In February 1951, after having lived for nearly a decade in Hollywood, California, Man Ray passed through New York on his return to Paris, and Duchamp came to the piers to see him off. In the privacy of his cabin, Duchamp handed him a small plaster sculpture that he had made a year earlier: one of the two original casts that he had made of his *Feuille de Vigne Femelle*. Man Ray, who spoke French fluently, would have been able to quickly translate the title, and we can only imagine that he must have been amused. Taken literally, a *Female Fig Leaf* would have been an object intended to cover the intimate body part of a woman, just as fig leaves had been used to cover the genitals of both male and female figures in antique statuary. This object, however, did not resemble a fig leaf, but looked like a plaster cast taken directly from the crotch of a woman; since it was a negative cast, it did not take a great leap of the imagination to envision this object returned to its place of origin, a snug fit that would not only cover the offending body part but also prevent any possible means of penetration, visual or physical.

Shortly after having completed the first two erotic objects, Duchamp added a third and final work to the trilogy, to which he gave the provocative title *Coin de Chasteté* (Wedge of Chastity; (Fig. 57). The item is comprised of a copper-electroplated plaster wedge embedded into an irregularly shaped mound of dental plastic. The title may have been intended as a direct reference to Duchamp's newfound fidelity, for he presented the object as a wedding gift to his wife Teeny. "We still have it on our table," Duchamp told an interviewer a few years later. "We usually take it with us, like a wedding ring." That this object was treated in this particular fashion may provide a clue to its meaning. Embedding an object into dental plastic simulates the procedure followed in the making of false teeth. Thus, by placing the object near their bedside table at night, Duchamp and his wife unwittingly duplicated the common practice of cleaning dental plates in a glass of

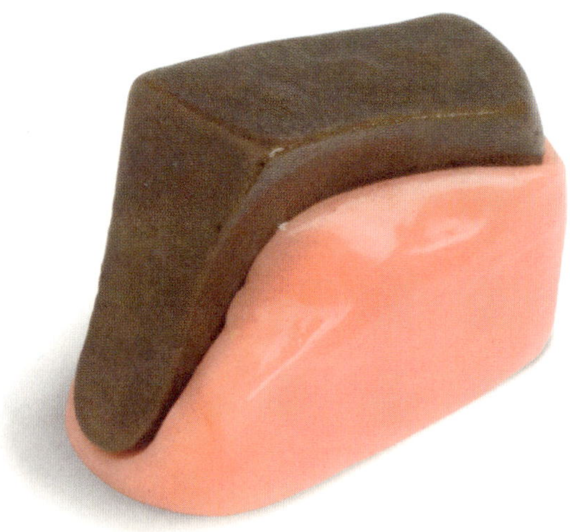

Fig. 57. Marcel Duchamp, *Coin de chasteté* (*Wedge of Chastity*), 1954. Sculpture in two sections, copper-electroplated plaster and dental plastic, 2 × 3⅜ × 1⅜ in. (5.1 × 8.6 × 3.5 cm). Private Collection.

water overnight, a ritual frequently associated with aging. "Growing old," Duchamp wrote to Walter Arensberg in a letter reporting his marriage, "the hermit plays devil." That very sense of the devious may have contributed to Duchamp's reason for calling this work *Wedge of Chastity*, for in presenting it to his wife as a wedding gift, he clearly referred to their fidelity, a position enforced—as securely as a chastity belt—by virtue of their old age.

In a series of exhibitions of Duchamp's works that were held in the early 1960s, the erotic objects were consistently represented as works produced in edition (rather than submit the originals, which were probably deemed too fragile to be subjected to the rigors of transport and display). The very fact that Duchamp produced these works in edition and allowed them to be exhibited so widely shows that he must have realized they created some intrigue about him and his work, while not giving away the secret of the environmental tableau he was still in the process of completing. With the continued display of these works and their reproduction in accompanying catalogues, however, it was no longer possible to ignore their existence. In 1966, Pierre Cabanne, who conducted the most extensive interview with Duchamp, was the first to ask him directly about them. The artist only described these objects in general terms, linking them to the general subject of eroticism, which, he acknowledged, permeated his work. "I believe in eroticism a lot," he said, "because it's truly a rather widespread thing throughout the world, a thought that everyone understands. It replaces, if you wish, what other literary schools call Symbolism, Romanticism. It could be another 'ism' so to speak." When Cabanne asked him to define eroticism,

Duchamp responded, "I don't give it a personal definition, but basically it's really a way to try to bring out in the daylight things that are constantly hidden—and that aren't necessarily erotic—because of the Catholic religion, because of social rules. To be able to reveal them, and to place them at everyone's disposal—I think this is important because it's the basis of everything, and no one talks about it."

All three of these erotic objects were shown in the Duchamp retrospective organized by the English artist Richard Hamilton for the Tate Gallery in London in 1966 and, in the accompanying catalogue, they were reproduced on the same page with a mysterious and then never-before-seen-or-known work by Duchamp called *Étant donnés le gaz d'éclairage et la chute d'eau*: the naked torso of a woman that Duchamp had given to Maria in 1949 (Fig. 49). In the catalogue, the dedication to Maria was transcribed, letting the whole world know that this work belonged to someone named Maria Martins, and that it was given to her "with affection." When it was seen by Duchamp hanging in the galleries (because of its subject matter, Hamilton displayed it next to the three erotic objects), the artist was visibly dismayed. "Where did you get that?" he asked Hamilton. "He was clearly very angry," Hamilton later recalled. "I somehow got the idea that I had betrayed him. But he offered no information about it, and he said nothing about removing it from the show." In an interview with the artist that was conducted in Hamilton's studio during the time of the exhibition, several people asked him about this strange construction and the three erotic objects, but he deflected their comments. When Hamilton asked him to explain his motives, he said "No[thing] special. Just a thing for her." (The "her" to whom he referred was not disclosed, but of course it was for Maria.) Also present at the interview was the art historian and critic David Sylvester, who asked if the *Female Fig Leaf* had been cast from life. "No," Duchamp responded. "It's not a cast. People think so, but it is not. It's modeling plaster," whereupon he curiously seemed to shift the conversation to his *Wedge of Chastity*. "I gave the original to my dentist, not even my dentist, but his mechanic. He asked $5 to make it and I gave him the plaster." Finally, Hamilton asked him flatly to explain the significance of the nude, and Duchamp's response was simply "Nothing."

At the time when these questions were being asked, virtually no one knew that the nude figure and the three erotic objects were all part of a major work that Duchamp had been working on in secrecy for twenty years and which he did not want to be placed on public display until after his death. In 1965, Duchamp learned that the lease was about to expire on the two rooms next to his studio on 14th Street where he was constructing the work, so he moved the tableau and all of its pieces to a rented office on East 11th Street, where he set it all up again and planned to make the finishing touches. The only people who had seen it near completion were Teeny and, as it turns out, Maria. She had visited New York in the spring of 1966, traveling alone this time, as her husband, Carlos, had died a year earlier at the age of eighty. She stayed at the home of Elba Sette Câmera, wife of a Brazilian delegate to the United Nations. To mark the occasion, a tea was organized in Maria's honor, to which Marcel was invited, as were a number of old friends whom Maria knew from her years in New York, including Alfred Barr, Jr., and James Johnson Sweeney of MoMA. According to a report filed by a Brazilian journalist who was also present, the group talked about the paintings that hung on the walls of the delegate's home, but nothing is known about any private conversation that might have taken place between Marcel and Maria. So far as we can tell, Marcel arrived at the party alone, and may very well have taken the opportunity to reminisce with Maria about their earlier years in New York. There is no reason to imagine that their exchange differed in any significant way from the friendly and respectful tone reflected in their last letters. We know that Marcel invited her to his storage room to see the *Étant donnés* completed. Indeed, since the work is signed and dated on the right arm of the nude *Marcel Duchamp 1946–66* (Fig. 58), it is tempting to speculate—as a scholar did recently in writing about this work—that Maria might have been present when the work was signed. We do not know what she thought of it, as there is no record of her reaction, but we can be fairly certain that she approved of the elaborate tableau he had devoted to her and assiduously constructed in secrecy for twenty years.

It is not known what else took place in this last meeting between the two former lovers. They had not seen each other for more than sixteen years. Marcel was now seventy-eight, Maria seventy-one. The earlier obstacle to her affection was no longer a factor (her marriage and social position as the wife of a diplomat were behind her), but this time the tables were turned: Duchamp was married, yet Maria remained the love of his life, the woman he had desired physically and emotionally from his youth, his *mariée*, a person to whom he

had given his heart unreservedly. Some comfort must
have come in their parting embrace, as he would have
told her that there were plans to place this elaborate
construction on display in the same galleries with his
other work at the Philadelphia Museum of Art after his
death. Thereby it would serve as long into the future as
a tribute to their enduring artistic and emotional bond.

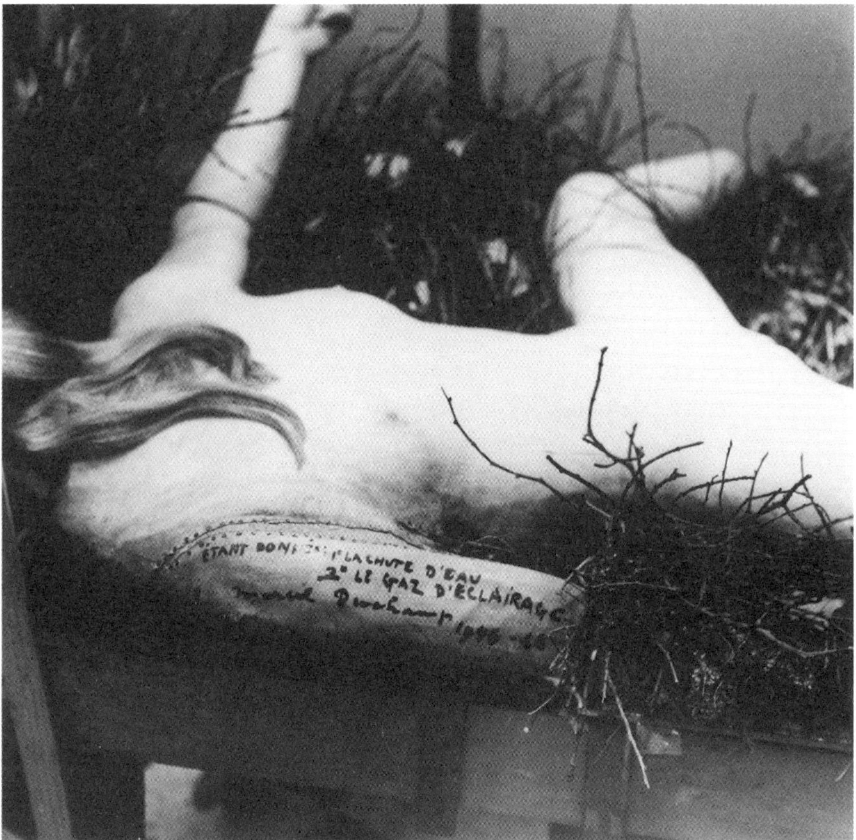

Fig. 58. Marcel Duchamp, inscription on the right arm of
the *Étant donnés* mannequin, 1966. Photograph by Denise Browne
Hare, 1968. Library and Archives, Philadelphia Museum of Art.

REVELATION

On July 7, 1969—about nine months after Duchamp died—the *Étant donnés: 1° la chute d'eau / 2° le gaz d'éclairage* (Given: 1° The Waterfall / 2° The Illuminating Gas; Figs. 59 and 60) opened to the public in the Philadelphia Museum of Art. In a gallery adjacent to where *The Large Glass* was placed on permanent display, viewers peered into two holes in the center of an antique wooden door and saw a naked female figure lying on a bed of twigs—her legs spread-eagled to reveal her exposed vulva for everyone to see. If you could get over the initial shock, you might then notice that to the right of the figure can be seen a running waterfall and, in her outstretched left hand, she holds a gas lamp, the two elements mentioned in the work's title: water and gas. Those intimately familiar with Duchamp's work would eventually figure out that there was a correlation between this work and *The Large Glass* (Fig. 19) in the next room, where these same two elements are not made visible but are nonetheless integral to its function as an elaborate lovemaking machine. Today more informed viewers might even peer out the window behind the glass looking for Maria's *Yara* (Fig. 6), but, unfortunately, the sculpture was damaged by an assailant in 1992 and has been moved into the museum for safekeeping. When the *Étant donnés* was placed on display, there was no formal opening, but almost immediately visitors to the museum began to notice the work and talk about it. Reactions varied. Their response was later summarized as "a pornographic howl," and Jasper Johns would declare the *Étant donnés* as "the strangest work of art any museum has ever had in it." For those who wanted to know more about this remarkable work of art, the *Bulletin* of the Philadelphia Museum of Art—which was released only five days before the work was placed on display—published a long and informative scholarly essay written by the museum's curator, Anne d'Harnoncourt, and her colleague, Walter Hopps.

It is in this publication that, for the first time, we learn that the nude study and the three erotic objects can be traced to this work. "The study is very close to the final work," they wrote of the relief sculpture that then still belonged to Maria Martins (Fig. 49), "delicately colored and modeled, with the important exceptions of the wave of blonde hair and the arm holding the lamp, which are not yet suggested." The *Objet-Dard* (Fig. 55) is described as having "the random look of part of a mold for something else," the *Female Fig Leaf* (Fig. 56) "almost suggests a cast from an impression of the *Étant donnés*," and *Wedge of Chastity* (Fig. 57) is only described as a wedding gift for Duchamp's wife that provides "a witty synthesis of the first two [erotic objects]." The authors then go on to quickly point out that although all three of these objects may look like molds or casts, they "were not taken from life." Some forty-three years would pass before we found out exactly

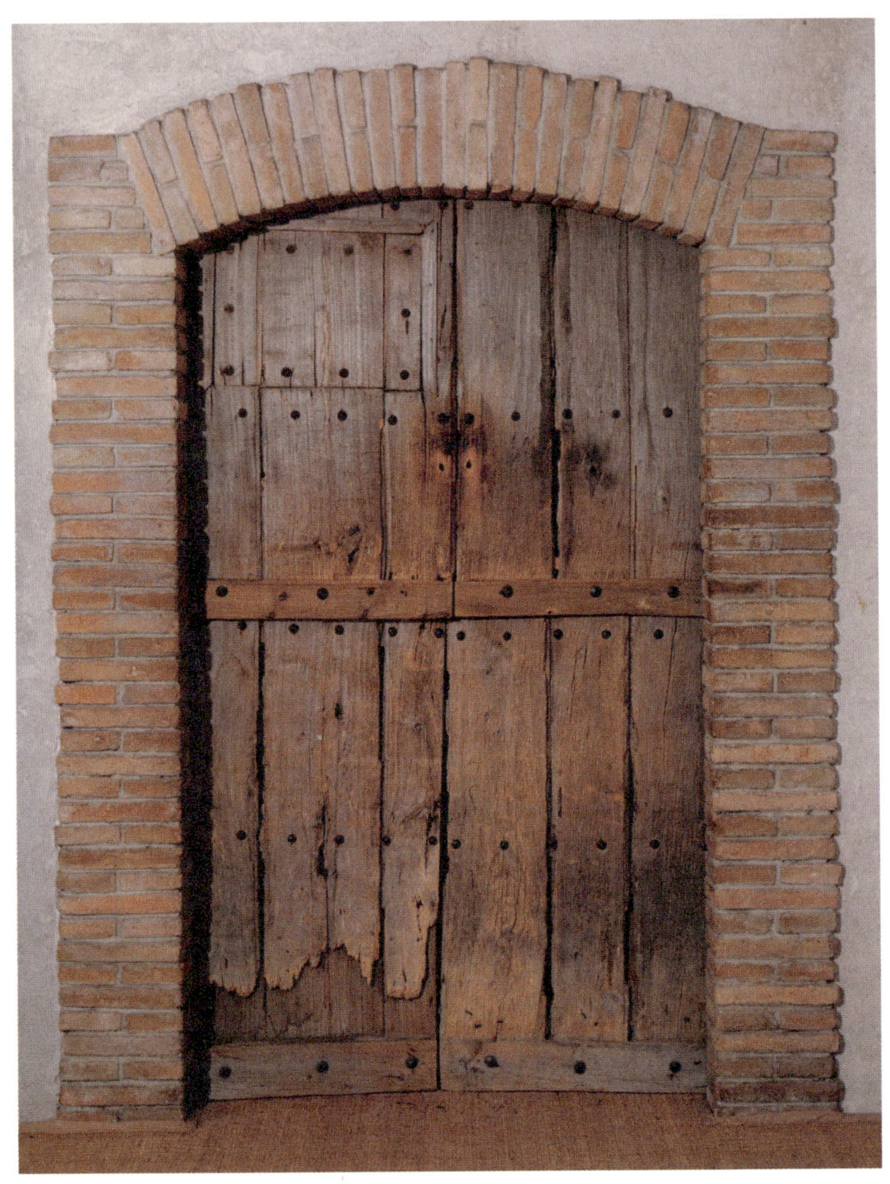

Fig. 59. Marcel Duchamp, *Étant donnés: 1° la chute d'eau, 2° le gaz d'élcairage* (Given: 1° the waterfall, 2° the illuminating gas), 1946–66, exterior. Philadelphia Museum of Art.

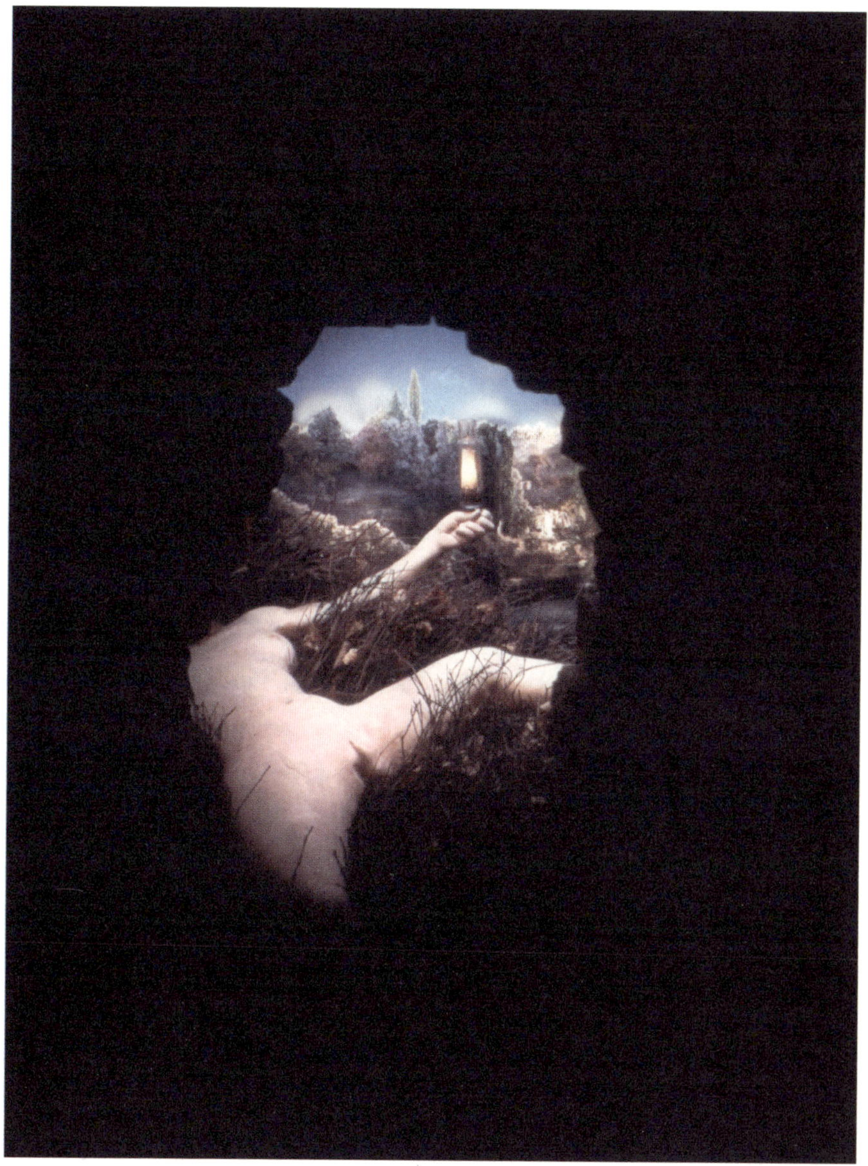

Fig. 60. Marcel Duchamp, *Étant donnés: 1° la chute d'eau, 2° le gaz d'élcairage* (Given: 1° the waterfall, 2° the illuminating gas), 1946–66, interior. Philadelphia Museum of Art.

where these objects originated, and that was only when a major exhibition on the *Étant donnés* was held at the Philadelphia Museum in 2009. The room in which the figure was enclosed was opened and found to contain several fragmentary studies for the figure. In examining these works, museum restorers discovered that the plaster casts of the *Female Fig Leaf* was not made from the figure in the tableau (as had been previously assumed), but rather from the crotch of one of these fragmentary studies, while the "wedge" for the *Wedge of Chastity* seems to have been made from another torso fabricated of parchment. The insertion of both of these objects into the studies was so effortless and snug that one could say—in paraphrasing Duchamp—they fit almost as well as "a penis is grasped by the vagina."

In having arranged for this last great work of art to be placed on public view after his death, Duchamp had taken his own advice to artists and gone underground, both literally (since he was buried in his family plot in Rouen) and metaphorically, since he would not be subjected to the reactions or criticism that the work—which was seemingly antithetical to anything else he had ever done before—was likely to generate. It was the equivalent of a strategic move in chess, one that a player hopes will go unnoticed by his opponent, but which will establish a position that leads to victory. Since it took place at the end of his life, it can be considered an endgame position, a final move in an artistic life that reflected the thoughtful strategy and precision that guided his moves on a chessboard.

ENDGAME

Maria would live only five more years after Duchamp's death. She experienced a rich and rewarding life, filled with exciting adventures from her teenage years to old age. In reflecting upon her professional life, she should have been proud of all she had accomplished. She continued to travel widely and wrote several books—one on China (1958), another on politics in the Middle East (1961), and one on Nietzsche (1965)—and she contributed a regular column to the *Correio da Manhã*, a leading newspaper in Rio. She participated regularly in the São Paulo Biennial, winning the Grand Prize for Sculpture in 1955, and in 1956 was given a retrospective at the Museum of Modern Art in Rio de Janeiro that was greeted with some controversy. The critics resented her years of absence from Brazil and attacked the overt sensuality and erotic nature of her work. One writer, Pedro Manuel, called it "obscene" and "lascivious," going so far as to claim it verged on the pornographic. "The mystery of reproductive fertilization is repeatedly depicted with infra-real satanic allegories," he wrote. "The content of the message is dirty."

Despite this sort of criticism, Maria was still considered among the most notable sculptors in Brazil. In

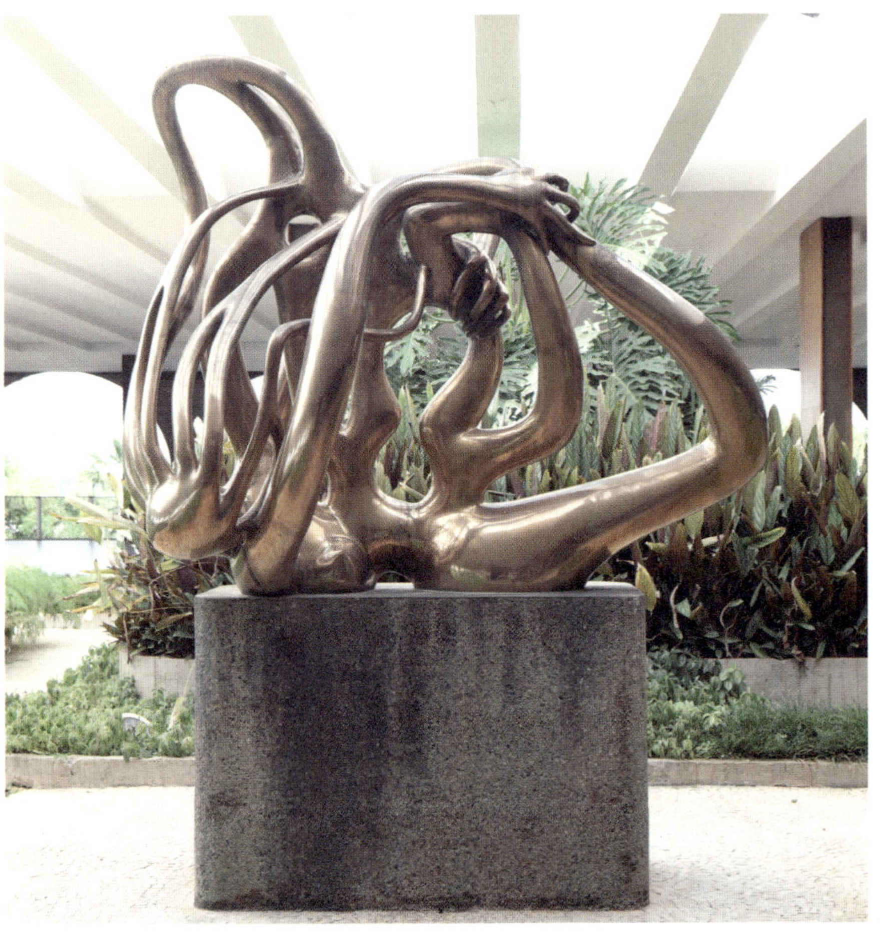

Fig. 61. Maria Martins, *Canto da noite*, 1968. Bronze, 65 × 78¾ × 42½ in. (165 × 200 × 108 cm). Collection Ministry of Foreign Affairs of Brazil, Palácio Itamaraty, Brasília. Photograph by Gustavo Magalhães.

1959, she was invited to design a monumental sculpture to be placed in front of the Palácio da Alvorada (Palace of Dawn) in Brasília, the new capital of the country. She completed *Tito do ritmo* (Rite of Rhythm), a bronze sculpture nearly seventeen feet tall, composed of intersecting forms that were likely derived from a human figure, but its high degree of abstraction was not understood by the general public. Nonetheless, it became the symbol of the new city and, in turn, of Brazil itself. In 1968, she was commissioned to make another sculpture to be placed before a palace in Brasília. This would be the last major work of her career, *Canto da noite* (Song of the Night; Fig. 61). At first, the sculpture appears to be entirely abstract, intertwining, curving shapes of polished bronze that seem to have been derived from the tropical vegetation of Brazil. Examining it more carefully, however, the viewer will see a pair of hands grasping these twisting forms. Followed to their source, they end in the torso of a nude female figure with outstretched legs. The gender is confirmed by an open gash that appears on a protuberance at the base (probably meant as a mouth, but because of its vertical orientation, serving a double purpose), around which emerge tentacles that rise upward and join one another at the top of the sculpture. These details have caused Graça Ramos to suggest that the sculpture might have been inspired by Maria's viewing of the *Étant donnés* when she visited New York two years earlier. The comparison is compelling, for she goes on to point out many other similarities between the two works. Both were derived from earlier work, in Duchamp's case from his *Large Glass* (Fig. 19), and in Maria's case her *I Believed That I Long Dreamed I Was Free* (Fig. 26), as it, too, depicts a nude female figure in polished bronze. As Maria's sculpture shows a woman entwined in foliage, Duchamp's nude lies on a bed of twigs, and, in both cases, the nudes are recumbent. "Just as *Étant donnés* summarizes Marcel Duchamp's oeuvre," Ramos concludes, "Maria Martins's last work, *Canto da noite*, synthesizes her artistic production."

Maria's relationship with Duchamp likely contributed significantly to her posthumous fame, although it came slowly in her own country and only after her death. She knew this might happen in her case, for as she wrote in her book on Nietzsche, "great thinkers and great artists are almost always disdained and denied by their generation." In that same book, she claimed that for all great artists, death should not be a concern. "For the true artist," she wrote, "destruction and death are irrelevant; the only thing that matters is creating, even if it is a bloody sacrifice. And creation can only exist when engendered by passion and revolt. And the passion of the artist-poet results in his vision and his ability to discern life in its essence and in its totality." When she died, in accordance with her wishes, Maria's body was dressed in a gold ball gown, and she wore no shoes, her faced covered by a veil. She asked for her veins to be drained of blood and filled with formaldehyde, as she feared being buried alive. "Death, after all, is the last thing, from which we cannot return," she told a journalist a few years before she died. "Despite everything, I think life is beautiful." When this same reporter asked what she would choose to be if she could live her whole life over again, she answered, "I would be an artist like I am, free and freed." As early as 1956, in another newspaper interview, she explained how a consciousness of her own mortality inspired her work: "I have a gypsy soul, and it would be profoundly unpleasant for me to have to set my feet on the ground, in a certain place, until the sight of death," to which she added, "After all, we don't die, it's others who die." Coincidentally (or perhaps not), those words are strikingly similar to those composed by Duchamp for the epitaph on his own tombstone: "Besides, it's always the others who die."

For her funeral, six of Maria's sculptures were placed around her coffin, and those who attended the wake were served shots of whisky. She left her mark on the country she loved, and we can be fairly certain that her sculpture shall continue to inspire young artists—not only Brazilians, but all those who come in contact with her work and read about her life—for generations to come.

AFTERMATH

The love affair between Marcel and Maria was unquestionably one of the most intense and important events to take place in either one of their lives. For a period of approximately eight years—from 1943 to 1951—they served as muses for one another, inspiring and encouraging each to create new works of art that were departures from what they made previously, and which would eventually leave their mark in the history of art. There was always more than a mere physical attraction to cause their minds and psyches to so intensely interlock. They did not even have to speak with each other to communicate; their work did that for them. Once we see the formal rapport that exists between the nude female figure in Maria's *I Believed That I Long Dreamed I Was Free* (Fig. 26a) and the similarly positioned figure Duchamp made for the *Étant donnés* (Fig. 60), we realize that images have their way of ingraining themselves in an artist's visual memory to freely resurface at a later date, a silent form of communication that has taken place in works of art ever since art existed. Their love burned brightly in their hearts for years, and clearly the memory of it could never be fully extinguished. For her part, the rapport that seems to exist between the *Étant donnés* and her last major sculpture, *Canto de noite* (Fig. 61), shows that the direction of influence continued to travel in both directions, long after their relationship was over. Finally, Maria's love affair with Duchamp inspired arguably the greatest single work of her career, *Impossible* (Figs. 23 and 24), its title alone indicating the degree of hopelessness and impracticality in their failed relationship.

Of course, the failure of their relationship raises the question: would their work have continued to be as powerful and meaningful had they never met? That question cannot be answered with any degree of confidence, for the results of hypotheticals are by their very nature impossible to determine with certainty. Maria might very well have continued making sculpture along the lines that she had before meeting Duchamp, but she may never have received the inspiration that only love can offer, nor would she have ever experienced the recognition that her affiliation with the Surrealist group provided, something that likely would not have happened without Duchamp's intercession. The impact of their relationship was clearly more significant on him, for he had never been in love before and, without it, he would not likely have found the inspiration to spend the last twenty years of his life creating his last great masterpiece. In the end, we as viewers are the beneficiaries of their relationship—failed or otherwise—an outcome both artists eventually became willing to accept. As Duchamp repeatedly explained in the final decades of his life, the audience completes a work of art by merely looking at it and thinking about what it means, and as history has proven, all great works of art endure long beyond the lives of their creators.

POSTSCRIPTUM

It is worthwhile devoting a few words to the negative reaction experienced by some when viewing the *Étant donnés* in the galleries of the Philadelphia Museum of Art for the first time. There are those who find the imagery disturbing and even pornographic: the body of a naked woman with her legs spread, exposing her to anyone who cares to look through two peepholes in an old wooden door installed against a gallery wall (Figs. 59 and 60). Besides, the figure is lying on dead branches, which to some reinforces the impression that she is dead, a body of a woman murdered, perhaps after a violent rape (most overlooking the fact that she holds a lantern in her upraised left hand). Whereas these are logical conclusions to draw, I believe that if the viewer were aware of the full story of its creation— that the *Étant donnés* is the end product of a profound *affair de coeur* between two individuals who genuinely loved each other, a relationship that not only deeply affected the creator of this work, but also work by the woman whose body is depicted within it—they would better understand its intent and, hopefully, react differently.

Rather than envision the nude as a hapless victim, they would understand that she cooperated fully with the artist in the realization of this work, posing for preparatory drawings (Figs. 34 and 40) and allowing her body to be cast in this knowingly compromised position (Fig. 50). In several letters to Maria Martins, Duchamp referred to the work as *N[otre] D[ame] des désirs* (Our Lady of Desires), not only alluding to the work in intentionally sacrilegious terms, but also using the word *notre* to underscore the fact that she was a willing accomplice in a work of art they were creating together. After all, depictions of female nudes in landscape settings fill museums throughout the world—Botticelli, Giorgione, Titian, Courbet, Manet, Picasso (to name but a few)—but in all of these cases we are presented with a scene from life rendered on the surface of a canvas. It could be argued that a percentage of the visual impact is lost through the process of translation, converting the image from one dimension to the other. In the case of the *Étant donnés*, however, we see an actual three-dimensional scene rendered in a dramatically naturalistic fashion, forcing viewers to confuse artifice for reality, clearly a reaction Duchamp desired.

In all of these earlier depictions of nudes in landscape settings, we are presented with a specifically male gaze at an unclothed female body, the model having had little to do with the way in which she was depicted. In contrast, Maria not only knew how she would be seen, but she willingly cooperated in the making of the work and, for all we know, might even have suggested and encouraged Duchamp in determining how she would be portrayed (contemporaneous prints and sculptures by her echo similar poses: Figs. 26a and 29). Maria's participation in the making of this work can only be properly assessed when we learn more about Marcel's relationship with her, information that is available, but only after we make an effort to become informed. (The same, it could be argued, is required for the comprehension of all great works of art.) Moreover, if the spectators understood this work as the visual manifestation of ideas that had preoccupied the artist in an essentially abstract construction made some thirty years earlier—namely, *The Large Glass*, which is on display in an adjacent gallery of the museum—they would better understand the *Étant donnés* as a work of art, and not just the inappropriate display of a naked woman, nor, for that matter, the product of some violent crime.

In regard to this latter reading, it should be acknowledged that a great deal of time and effort has been devoted to linking the *Étant donnés* to the Black Dahlia murder case, a famous unsolved crime that took place in Los Angeles in 1947 and has been the subject of several books and films. A number of authors have claimed that crime-scene photographs of the naked, dismembered body of the murder victim, Elizabeth Short, a twenty-two-year-old aspiring actress then working as a waitress in Hollywood, resemble images of the *Étant donnés*, thereby implying that Duchamp was inspired by them. The main problem with this theory is that the artist could never have seen those photographs, as they were not made public until the late 1990s, not only long after this work was conceived, but long after Duchamp's death. Moreover, we know that the artist dated the *Étant donnés* to "1946–66" (Fig. 58), as he was accounting for the fact that the first drawing made for it is dated 1946 (Fig. 34), a year *before* the Black

Dahlia murder took place. What added fuel to this farfetched theory is that one suspect in the murder was later revealed to be a physician by the name of George Hodel, a highly disreputable character who had his portrait taken by the photographer Man Ray, a friend of Duchamp's. This caused subsequent authors to believe that Man Ray, who was then living in Hollywood, and his dealer, William N. Copley, had special access to these crime-scene pictures and to suggest (without offering any evidence) that they were shared with Duchamp. Of course we know that drawing conclusions from visual comparisons is the modus operandi of all art historians, but when their deductions are this preposterous—that Duchamp placed the body of his mannequin in a position to resemble that of a grisly murder scene—they deserve to be challenged and categorically dismissed, as, thankfully, they have been in recent years by several art historians. Of course conspiracy theories such as these are impossible to fully eradicate, because the general public is attracted to their sensationalism, which, unfortunately, holds a greater allure for many than the actual facts of what took place.

When Duchamp's affair with Maria Martins occurred in the 1940s, he had already dropped out of the art world, many assuming that he had done so in order to devote himself to the game of chess. Whereas this is true to a certain extent, more than for any other reason Duchamp ceased actively creating and exhibiting his work because he did not wish to repeat himself. "The idea of repeating myself," he later told an interviewer, "is a form of masturbation." Certainly we know that he had nothing against the practice, particularly when it came to his relationship with Maria Martins

(Fig. 20). What he meant, however, is that he did not want to replicate works he had already made just to attain fame and fortune in the art world, as he believed many of his more financially successful contemporaries had done. Indeed, he came to the conclusion that many artists were no longer making paintings, but just engaged in the process of writing checks and, thereby, reaping the benefit of their own repetition. If he created a new work of art, it would have to be completely different from anything he had done before, which, more than any other factor, inspired the form taken by his *Étant donnés*, as it did not resemble anything he had made previously.

Indeed, it is the visual disconnect between the *Étant donnés* and the work Duchamp made earlier in his career that presents the greatest obstacle to some viewers, as they are incapable of reconciling this three-dimensional tableau with the work the artist was best known for. Many who have come to accept the importance of Duchamp's central contribution to the art of the modern era—his introduction of the concept of the readymade—have had difficulty in accepting this acutely naturalistic work as part of his legacy, something that conceptually makes no sense within the the oeuvre of an artist who had earlier challenged the very definition of art and changed its history. The *Étant donnés* seems to be precisely the opposite of anything like that, since it revives a desire to simulate reality, which had been considered the goal of most academic art since the Renaissance. Just as the readymade had altered our perceptions of art, however, this new work would result in altering our perceptions of Duchamp. This might have been precisely what he intended, but he would not be around to witness any reactions—positive or negative—since he ingeniously arranged for the work to be placed on public display only after his death. In the present text I have likened this strategy to a great move in a chess game (p. 136), one that eludes the perception of your opponent and, therefore, results in the artist's ultimate victory.

Finally, another factor that contributes significantly to how viewers perceive this work today is a result of presentism, that is, attempting to comprehend and assess works of the past by today's moral standards, which differ significantly from those at the time when the work was conceived and made. Of course, nothing that has been said fully refutes the legitimate objections raised by feminists—both male and female—who perceive the *Étant donnés* as misogynistic, a visual violation of womankind. Nevertheless, it is hoped that with a greater understanding of its origins, viewers can come to understand this work as the equivalent of a visual love letter locked in a box, the result of a deep emotional bond that inspired two artists to create radically new and important work that differed significantly from anything they—or for that matter, anyone else—had ever done before.

BIBLIOGRAPHIC NOTE

Since my first investigation of the subject of this book took place in the early 1990s, much information about the two artists who are its protagonists—Marcel Duchamp and Maria Martins—has been published. (For complete citations see the bibliography below.) The field of Duchamp scholarship has virtually exploded over that time, beginning with the exceptionally well-written and researched biography by Calvin Tomkins (not only the original edition that appeared in 1996, but also the revised and expanded edition published by the Museum of Modern Art in New York in 2014), and also the third and final edition of the massive Duchamp catalogue raisonné compiled by Arturo Schwarz (1997). Specific to the subject at hand is the magisterial catalogue written by Michael R. Taylor that accompanied the *Étant donnés* exhibition he organized for the Philadelphia Museum of Art in 2009, where not only is the conception and construction of the work thoroughly documented, but the thirty-five extant letters written by Duchamp to Martins were translated into English and published for the first time. Whereas I knew about the existence of these letters and had photocopies, I was prohibited from publishing them, as the daughter of Maria Martins and the Duchamp estate then considered their contents too intimate and private for publication.

Since my catalogue on the work of Maria Martins that accompanied an exhibition at the Emmerich Gallery in 1998, the various publications on the artist that have come out of South America have been equally voluminous. The first is a biography of Maria by Ana Arruda Callado that was in Portuguese and published in 2004, followed by a book written by the Argentine scholar Raúl Antelo that appeared in Spanish in 2006, devoted to exploring the relationship between the work of Duchamp and Martins. Both of these authors had only limited access to the Duchamp letters, so they were unaware of the full extent of their emotional and artistic involvement. Clearly the most important and informative text on the work of Maria Martins is the monograph on the artist by Graça Ramos, which appeared in 2009 (written in Portuguese, but, thankfully, with English translations at the back of the book), followed in 2010 by a collection of essays in English edited by Charles Cosac with a detailed chronology. The catalogue by Veronica Stigger that accompanied a retrospective exhibition at the Museu de Arte Moderna in São Paulo in 2013 was also most helpful, especially for its translations into English of Maria's writings of the late 1960s for *Correio da Manhã*. Finally, in 2017 a major documentary film on Maria's art and life was released in Brazil. Called *Maria: Don't Forget I Come from the Tropics*, directed by Elisa Gomes and Francisco C. Martins (no relation to Maria), it featured interviews with individuals who knew the artist, as well as art historians in America and Brazil who have specialized in her work.

As notes to the present volume openly acknowledge, I have freely consulted all these sources for information on the artist and her writings that would not have otherwise been available to me.

BIBLIOGRAPHY

Antelo, Raúl. *Maria con Marcel: Duchamp en los Trópicos*. Buenos Aires: Siglo XXI Editores Argentina, 2006.

Callado, Ana Arruda. *Maria Martins: Uma biografia*. Brasília: Gryphus, 2004.

Cosac, Charles, ed. *Maria*. Photographs by Vicente de Mello. Contributions by Francis M. Naumann, Dawn Ades, Jossé Resende, and Veronica Stigger. 2 vols. São Paulo: Ipsis, 2010.

Naumann, Francis M. *Maria: The Surrealist Sculpture of Maria Martins*. New York: André Emmerich Gallery, 1998.

———. "The Bachelor's Quest." Art in America 81, no. 9 (September 1993): 67–69, 72–81.

———. "Marcel & Maria." Art in America 89, no. 4 (April 2001): 98–111, 157.

Ramos, Graça. *Maria Martins: Escultora dos Trópicos*. São Paulo: Artviva, 2009.

Rjeille, Isabella, ed. *Maria Martins: Tropical Fictions*. Contributions by Alyce Majon, Beverly Adams, Fernanda Lopes, and others. Museu de Arte de São Paulo, 2022.

Schwarz, Arturo. *The Complete Works of Marcel Duchamp*. New York: Harry N. Abrams, 1968. 3rd rev. and expanded ed. New York: Delano Greenidge Editions, 1999.

Stigger, Veronica. *Maria Martins: Metamorfoses*. Museu de Arte Moderna de São Paolo, 2013.

Taylor, Michael R. *Étant donnés*, Philadelphia Museum of Art, 2009.

———. "Don't Forget I Come from the Tropics: Reconsidering the Surrealist Sculpture of Maria Martins." *Journal of Surrealism and the Americas* 8, no. 1 (2014): 74–89.

Tomkins, Calvin. *Duchamp: A Biography*. New York: Henry Holt and Company, 1996. 2nd rev. ed. New York: Museum of Modern Art, 2014.

NOTES

Page

11   "Tell me who your enemies are . . . " Nora Lobo, the
daughter of Maria Martins, said that she could see her
mother saying these words when introducing herself
to someone, although she did not say they were the words
used when she met Duchamp (Calvin Tomkins, *Duchamp:
A Biography* [New York: Henry Holt and Company, 1996],
p. 355; 2nd rev. ed. [New York: Museum of Modern Art,
2014], p. 351; all subsequent references to this publication
are to the second edition).

11   "a small, dark-haired, vibrantly attractive woman,"
Calvin Tomkins, *Duchamp: A Biography*, p. 348. Tomkins
mistakenly said that Maria was "thirteen years younger
than [Duchamp]" (p. 349). Duchamp was born in 1887,
Maria in 1894, so there was only a seven-year age difference between them.

15   "he left me his indomitable passion . . . ," from the dedication page of Maria Martins, *Asia Maior: Brama, Gandhi
e Nehru* (1961); cited in Graça Ramos, *Maria Martins:
Escultora dos Trópicos* (São Paulo: Artviva, 2009), p. 209.
Maria's early interest in classical music is relayed in
an interview with the newspaper *O Jornal* (Rio de Janeiro),
November 9, 1958, p. 7. (I am grateful to Raúl Antelo
for having provided me with a copy of this article)

17   For more on Maria's interest in the myths and folklore
of the Amazon rainforest, see Michael R. Taylor, *"Don't
Forget I Come from the Tropics*: Reconsidering the Surrealist
Sculpture of Maria Martins," *Journal of Surrealism and
the Americas* 8, no. 1 (2014), pp. 74–80.

19   "mythological figures of the Amazon region . . . ," in
"Madame Carlos Martins," *Vogue*, April 1, 1943, pp. 60–61.

19–21   The texts in *Amazonia* are unsigned, but in 1959 Maria
        acknowledged that she was their author; see Charles
        Cosac, "Chronology," in *Maria*, vol. 2 (São Paulo: Ipsis,
        2010), p. 292, n. 25, and p. 293.

21–22   On the Philadelphia Museum of Art's acquisition of
        Yara, see Michael R. Taylor, *Étant donnés* (Philadelphia
        Museum of Art, 2009), p. 28.

22   The scrapbook that contains a photograph of *Yara* is
        preserved in the collection of Portia Jones, Philadelphia,
        Pennsylvania; it is reproduced in Taylor, *"Don't Forget I
        Come from the Tropics,"* fig. 2. It is also possible that, on one
        of these visits to Maria's studio, she told Duchamp that
        her large wood sculpture depicting St. Francis was
        purchased by the Metropolitan Museum in New York in
        1942 (see "Metropolitan Buys Brazilian Sculpture,"
        New York Times, May 10, 1942, p. 37).

24   Part of the story of Maria's purchase of the Mondrian is
        recounted by Ana Arruda Callado (see Cosac, *ibid*, p. 293,
        n. 27), but Nora Lobo also told me that the painting was
        hand-carried by Duchamp and Maria to the museum con-
        versation, São Paulo, Brazil, 1997.

24–25   "the first to express great enthusiasm . . . ," Amédée
        Ozenfant, untitled statement written for the catalogue of
        the exhibition *Maria: Esculturas*, Museu de Arte Moderna,
        São Paulo, 1950; in English in Naumann, *Maria: The
        Surrealist Sculpture of Maria Martins*, (New York: André
        Emmerich Gallery, 1998), p. 51. Portions of the present text
        are freely derived from that publication.

25   "Maria has succeeded marvelously . . . ," André Breton,
        "Maria," introduction to *Maria: Recent Sculptures*, (New
        York: Julien Levy Gallery, 1947); reprinted in Breton,
        Le Surréalisme et la peinture (Paris: Gallimard, 1965); English
        trans. by Simon Watson Taylor, *Surrealism and Painting*
        (London: Macdonald, 1972), p. 320.

28   "The rococo . . . ," Howard Devree, "Diverse One-Man
        Shows," *New York Times*, May 14, 1944, Art-Auctions
        Section, p. 7.

28   "the last living manifestation . . . ," Clement Greenberg,
        "Review of a Group Exhibition at the Art of this Century
        Gallery and of Exhibitions of Maria Martins and Luis
        Quintanilla," *The Nation*, May 27, 1944; reprinted in
        John O'Brian, ed. *Clement Greenberg: The Collected Essays*

and Criticism, vol. 1: *Perceptions and Judgments, 1939–1944* (University of Chicago Press, 1986), p. 210.

30 "Her jewels coin emotion in metal . . . ," "Sculptress-Jeweller [*sic*], Maria," *Vogue*, July 1, 1944, p. 95.

31 Nora Lobo recalled her father's attitude toward her mother's affairs in Tomkins, *Duchamp*, p. 351.

31–34 On the studio rental, see Jennifer Gough-Cooper and Jacques Caumont, "Ephemerides," in Pontus Hulten, ed., *Marcel Duchamp* (Cambridge, MA: MIT Press, 1993), entry for October 1, 1943. A journalist who visited Duchamp in this studio a few years later reported that his rent had been raised to $40 per month; see Winthrop Sargeant, "Dada's Daddy," *Life* 32, no. 17 (April 28, 1952), p. 108.

34–35 "the attitude of combating invasion . . . ," from "The European Art Invasion," *The Literary Digest* 51, no. 22 (November 27, 1915), p. 1225. After the war, when Duchamp was asked if the conflict might have influenced the development of the arts, he was even more blunt. "I don't mix potatoes with shit," he wrote in response to a questionnaire published in Curnonsky, ed., with caricatures by George de Zayas, *Huit Peintres, Deux Sculpteurs, et un Musicien très moderne* (Paris: printed privately, 1919), n.p.

35 On Maria's disinterest in politics, see Maria Martins, "Poeira da vida," *Correio da Manhã*, October 27, 1968, reprinted in Veronica Stigger, ed., *Maria Martins: Metamorfoses* (Museu de Arte Moderna de São Paulo, 2013), p. 288.

35 "*Cela n'a pas d'importance*," quoted in Beatrice Wood, "Marcel," in Rudolf E. Kuenzli and Francis M. Naumann, eds., *Marcel Duchamp: Artist of the Century* (Cambridge, MA: MIT Press, 1987), pp. 13, 16–17.

36–39 For more on the valise, see Ecke Bonk, *Marcel Duchamp The Box in a Valise: de ou par Marcel Duchamp ou Rrose Sélavy* (New York: Rizzoli, 1989); Bonk mistakenly gives the date of the opening of the Peggy Guggenheim exhibition as October 1941 (p. 258), but then gives it correctly in his chronology as October 1942 (pp. 166–67). For a narrative history of this work, see Naumann, "Valise and Box in a Valise," *The Recurrent, Haunting Ghost: Essays on the Art, Life and Legacy of Marcel Duchamp* (New York: Readymade Press, 2012), chapter 14, pp. 136–157. The photograph of Duchamp with the valise appeared in "Artist Descending to America," *Time*, September 7, 1942, p. 102.

39   "The son must hate the father . . . ," quoted in Laurie Eglington, "Marcel Duchamp, Back in America, Gives Interview," *Art News* 32 (November 18, 1933), p. 11.

39   "There is no alternative in art . . . ," Maria Martins, "The Biennial and Itamarati," *Correio da Manhã*, October 29, 1967; quoted in Stigger, *Metamorfoses*, p. 275.

40   "This is the great danger of liberation . . . ," Martins wrote this statement for inclusion in her catalogue, *Les Statues magiques de Maria* (Paris: Galerie René Drouin, 1948), no. 20; quoted in Ramos, *Maria Martins*, pp. 234, 260. She was here describing her work *La femme a perdu son ombre* (The Woman Who Lost Her Shadow), which dates from 1946, although it is possible that the ideas that inspired it were formulated earlier.

40   The date of the Julien Levy exhibition has long been given incorrectly, following information provided in the catalogue raisonné by Arturo Schwarz, *The Complete Works* (1968), cat. 329, p. 523; 3rd ed. (1999), cat. 530, p. 793. Since Schwarz gave this exhibition a date of 1948, the information was regrettably repeated in the otherwise reliable chronology prepared by Anne d'Harnoncourt in *Marcel Duchamp* (New York: Museum of Modern Art; Philadelphia Museum of Art, 1973), p. 25. In his account of the exhibition, Julien Levy gave the date correctly as December 7–28, 1943; see his *Memoir of an Art Gallery* (New York: G. P. Putnam's Sons, 1977), p. 309. Recently, this date has been confirmed by three contemporary reviews: "Modernism," *New York Times*, December 12, 1943, p. 8; "From the Passing Shows," *Art News* 42, no. 15 (December 15–31, 1943), p. 29; and "Give Art for Christmas—Bargains in Beauty," *The Art Digest* 18, no. 6 (December 15, 1943).

42   "There is no solution . . ." is a remark by Duchamp first recorded in Harriet and Sidney Janis, "Marcel Duchamp: Anti-Artist," *View*, series 5, no. 1 (March 1945), p. 24, and repeated in Winthrop Sargeant, "Dada's Daddy," *Life* 52, no. 17 (April 28, 1952), p. 111.

42   My analysis of the endgame problem first appeared in Naumann, "A Problem with No Solution," *The Sienese Shredder*, no. 1 (Winter 2006–7), pp. 180–87.

43   Duchamp uses the word "cage" to describe their relationship in several letters to Maria; see those of April 7 and June 20 [1949]; trans. Paul Edwards, in Taylor, *Étant donnés*, p. 409, 413.

46 *Piet Mondrian*, Museum of Modern Art, New York, March 21–May 13, 1945. Hanging at left in this installation shot is *Trafalgar Square*, which was painted in London in 1939, but reworked in New York in 1943.

48–49 Maria's first husband was Octávio Tarquinio de Souza (1889–1958), who went on to become a well-known historian in Brazil. It was Nora Lobo who told me about her mother's affair with Mussolini, but she forbade me to publish it in the catalogue I was working on at the time for the Emmerich Gallery in New York. The information has since been published online: "Maria Martins," *D.C. Writers' Homes*, https://dcwritershomes.wdchumanities.org/maria-martins/; and Penny Peace, "Monument Mondays—Maria Martins," *Suffrage Forward*, https://www.suffrageforward.org/blog-monumentmondays/monument-mondays-maria-martins.

49 For more on Reynolds's life, see the biography by Christine Oddo, *Mary Reynolds: Artiste surréaliste et amant de Marcel Duchamp* (Paris: Tallandier, 2021).

50 Duchamp later relayed the incident of having seen his daughter to his wife, Teeny; see Cooper and Caumont, "Ephemerides," entry for June 23, 1966.

50 "a narrow escape . . . ," see Taylor, *Étant donnés*, p. 29, who cites as his source Alan G. Wilkinson, *The Sculpture of Jacques Lipchitz: A Catalogue Raisonné*, vol. 2, *The American Years, 1941–1973* (New York: Thames and Hudson, 2000), cat. 369.

51 On *Paysage fautif*, see William A. Camfield, *Marcel Duchamp Fountain*, (Houston: Menil Collection, 1989), cat. no. 12. The medium is not given there, but is disclosed in Ecke Bonk, *Marcel Duchamp: The Box in a Valise* (New York: Rizzoli, 1989), p. 282.

53 "The bachelor grinds his chocolate . . . ," see Michel Sanouillet and Elmer Peterson, eds., *Salt Seller: The Writings of Marcel Duchamp (Marchand du Sel)* (New York: Oxford University Press, 1973), p. 51 , n. 11; on the Bachelors grinding their own chocolate, see p. 68, n. 21.

53 "Marcel must have enjoyed . . . ," Julien Levy quoted in Anne d'Harnoncourt, "Visit to Julien Levy," February 24, 1973, Philadelphia Museum of Art Archives, Marcel Duchamp Exhibition Records (quoted in Taylor, *Étant donnés*, p. 29).

56   "Works of art . . . ," Rilke quoted in *MARIA: NEW SCULPTURES* (New York: Valentine Gallery, 1946). The quote originally misprinted *armour* [armor] for *amour* [love], which has been corrected here.

59   Maria's poem comes from an undated manuscript page (Collection Katia Midlin Leite Barbosa, Rio de Janeiro, Brazil).

60   "There was a time when . . . ," Edward Alden Jewell, "Art: Hither and Yon," *New York Times*, April 28, 1946, Art section, p. 6. Jewell also explained that *Saudade* "refers to a kind of nostalgia that is, in Maria's own phrase, 'like a bell in your heart'"

61   I am grateful to James W. McManus, who identified this portrait (Fig. 25) as a photograph taken by Ethel Pries.

61–63   "Maria's most startling new efforts . . . ," "Underground Art," *Time*, May 6, 1946.

62–63   The sculpture (Fig. 26) was acquired by the Davis Museum at Wellesley College in 1948. At some point in the 1950s or 1960s, it was placed outside at the edge of a pond on the campus, where it was subsequently vandalized and thrown into the water. A fragment of the figure's body has been recovered, but efforts to locate the rest of the sculpture have not proven fruitful.

64   On Pollock's desire to be a sculptor, see Steven Naifeh and Gregory White Smith, *Jackson Pollock: An American Saga* (New York: Clarkson N. Potter, 1989), pp. 243, 608.

65   "to give surreal effects of transparency . . . ," Martica Sawin, "Stanley William Hayter at 84," *Arts* 60, no. 5 (January 1986), p. 60. For more on Hayter and his years in New York, see Deborah Rosenthal, "Stanley William Hayter," in *Stanley William Hayter in America: Paintings, Drawings and Prints 1940–1950* (New York: Francis M. Naumann Fine Art, 2009).

65   The text of Maria's "Explication" is given in English in Naumann, *The Surrealist Sculpture of Maria Martins*, 1998, pp. 46–48.

68   "a mirror, a lamp, a comb . . . ," Ramos, *Maria Martins*, p. 243.

69   "Despite everything you tell yourself . . . ," Marcel to Maria, undated but estimated to be written in 1946 (Taylor, *Étant donnés*, p. 404–5).

70   That Duchamp traveled to Paris to negotiate the acquisition works for the Museum of Modern Art is reported in Tomkins, *Duchamp*, p. 354.

70   "I have not yet detected the slightest echo . . . ," Duchamp to Martins, May 12, 1946 (Taylor, *Étant donnés*, p. 405).

73   The word *arrivée* as possibly referring to sexual climax was suggested by Taylor, *Étant donnés*, p. 30.

73–76   The description of this note closely follows that in Naumann, "Marcel & Maria," *Art in America* 89, no. 4 (April 2001), p. 105; transcriptions and translations of these notes are in Naumann, *The Recurrent, Haunting Ghost: Essays on the Art, Life and Legacy of Marcel Duchamp* (New York: Readymade Press, 2012), pp. 166–67. In these essays, I mistakenly said that the capillary tubes emanate from the heads of the bachelors, when in actual fact they can be traced to their midsections—what Duchamp called their "plane of sex"—a far more meaningful position for the point I am trying to make. (See his diagram for the *Nine Malic Molds*, in Arturo Schwarz ed., *Notes and Projects for the Large Glass* [New York: Harry N. Abrams, 1970], p. 145, n. 91.)

73   The Duchamp scholar who referred to this note as "a coded love letter" was Linda Henderson (in conversation, April 2000). Henderson is the author of a major book on *The Large Glass* and its scientific sources, *Duchamp in Context: Science and Technology in the* Large Glass *and Related Works* (Princeton, NJ: Princeton University Press, 1998); see also the revised and expanded edition (2005).

77   "The erotic act . . . ," from a letter to Serge Stauffer, May 28, 1961; quoted in Stauffer, *Marcel Duchamp: Die Schriften*, vol. 1 (Zurich: Regenbogen-Verlag, 1981), pp. 265–66. I first proposed Duchamp's use of optics as a means to render the fourth dimension, and its reference to the erotic content of *The Large Glass* in Naumann, "Optics," chap. 13, *The Recurrent, Haunting Ghost*, pp. 120–35.

77   "more cerebral than physical," Nora Lobo quoted in Tomkins, *Duchamp*, p. 351.

78   "as gentle in bed," Beatrice Wood quoted in Naumann, "Marcel & Maria," p. 110.

78   For a facsimile of the *Étant donnés* note providing a complete title, see Schwarz, *Notes and Projects for the Large Glass*, pp. 182–83, n. 124.

80   I am grateful to Thomas Girst for having drawn my attention to the foot in Ingres's painting. If Duchamp's drawing of the underside of a foot was made in Paris, this comparison is all the more compelling, since it is possible that the

two artists might have seen the Ingres painting together on a visit to the Louvre.

82   Mary Reynolds knew the Hoppenots through their daughter Violaine, who, with Mary, had become active in the French Resistance during the war.

83–84   "Mary herself is hardly cheerful . . . ," in Mary Reynolds and Hélène Hoppenot, "Confidences: un dialogue à travers les lettres de Mary Reynolds et le journal intime d'Hélène Hoppenot," *Étant donné Marcel Duchamp*, no. 8 (2007), diary entry of September 7, 1947, p. 124; quoted in Paul B. Franklin, "In the Beginning, There Was Mary: Marcel Duchamp, Mary Reynolds, and the Landscape Backdrop of *Étant donnés*," in Stefan Banz, ed., *Marcel Duchamp and the Forestay Waterfall* (Zurich: JRP/Ringier, 2010), p. 77.

86   Since this drawing (Fig. 40) is dated December 1947, and because it has always been considered the first drawing for the *Étant donnés* (which Duchamp himself dated 1946–1966), Michael Taylor feels that it was actually made in 1946 and only given to Maria Martins in 1947 (see Taylor, *Étant donnés*, pp. 66–67). I believe Duchamp assigned the *Étant donnés* a beginning date of 1946 because he knew that the first sketch he had made for it—the drawing of Maria's foot (Fig. 34)—was from that year. He may also have made other sketches in that year that do not survive, even though Maria (to whom Duchamp had given the drawing) believed it was the first sketch for the *Étant donnés*, as confirmed in a letter that she wrote to Evan Turner, Director of the Philadelphia Museum of Art, in 1969 (cited in Taylor, *Étant donnés*, p. 66 and pp. 120–21, n. 21). I do not believe a change in the dating of this drawing is necessary, for Duchamp was characteristically quite precise in dating his work, being careful to record the date when it was made, even when it was given as a gift to a friend at a later time.

85–87   "The view is frontal . . . ," Tomkins, *Duchamp*, p. 353.

88   "She was very much in love with Duchamp," quoted in Ramos, *Maria Martins*, p. 231.

88   The hair in the charm bracelet was first observed by Donald Joint, an artist who examined the piece in Miami, Florida, in December 2013.

90   "She [Maria] was madly in love with Duchamp. . . ," from an interview with Michael Taylor, New York, December 14, 2006 (quoted in Taylor, *Étant donnés*, pp. 65–66). I, too, interviewed Donati at his studio in the 1990s, and he told

me that "Maria was just a hanger-on," and he felt she was only with Duchamp to promote her own career as an artist.

91   "She is really charming . . . ," Yves Tanguy, *Lettres de Loin à Marcel Jean* (Paris: Le Dilettante, 1993), p. 73. I am grateful to Stephen Robeson-Miller for having drawn this reference to my attention.

94   "I never thought . . . ," from an interview with Michael Taylor, December 14, 2006 (Taylor, *Étant donnés*, p. 70). As Taylor points out, in his interview with Pierre Cabanne, Duchamp downplayed Donati's role in this entire project (ibid., p. 121 , n. 35).

94   On the installation of this exhibition, see Marcel Jean, *The History of Surrealist Painting* (New York: Grove Press, 1967), p. 342.

98   For Duchamp's description of Maria's work, see his interview with James Johnson Sweeney, November 24, 1945, where he says "Maria: non-retinian + acoustical" (Philadelphia Museum of Art, Alexina and Marcel Duchamp Papers). I have taken the liberty of changing the word "retinian" to "retinal," which I believe is what Duchamp meant (and might actually have said, as there survives only a transcript of their interview); see also Taylor, *"Don't Forget I Come from the Tropics,"* p. 86.

99   "owes nothing to the sculpture of the past . . . ," André Breton, "Maria," introduction to *Maria: Recent Sculptures* (New York: Julien Levy Gallery, 1947) reprinted in Breton, *Surréalisme et la peinture* (Paris: Gallimard, 1965); English trans. Simon Watson Taylor, *Surrealism and Painting* (London: Macdonald, 1972), p. 320.

99–100   "more clearly plastic manifestation . . . ," Howard Devree, "Exotics of the Week," *New York Times*, November 30, 1947, Art section, p. 12.

100   "No other sculptress . . . ," "Reviews and Previews: Maria," *Art News* 46, no. 10 (December 1947), p. 43.

100   "Art exists only as an individual expression . . . ," Maria Martins, *Módulo: revista de arquitetura e artes plásticas* (Rio de Janeiro,) 2, no. 4 (March 1956); cited in Ramos, *Maria Martins*, p. 201.

101   "It was by the destruction of works of art . . . ," Maria Martins, "Art, Liberation and Peace," in Penelope Rosemont, ed., *Surrealist Women: An International Anthology* (London: Athlone Press, 1998), pp. 217–18. I am grateful to Victoria Gelfand-Magalhaes for having drawn this

    citation to my attention. See also *Congressional Record–House*, June 18, 1947, p. 7252 (https://www.congress.gov/80/crecb/1947/06/18/GPO-CRECB-1947-pt6-5.pdf).

101 "I don't believe in art . . . ," quoted in "Art Was a Dream," *Newsweek*, November 9, 1959, p. 118. Although the interviewer is not acknowledged in the magazine, it was Calvin Tomkins.

103 "Nothing will change our love . . . ," Duchamp to Maria, August 17 [1948] (Taylor, *Étant donnés*, p. 407).

103 "These 8 days in the country . . . ," Duchamp to Martins, September 6 [1948] (Taylor, *Étant donnés*, pp. 407, 409).

104 "In case of restoration or framing . . . ," for full transcription and translation, see Schwarz, *Complete Works*, cat. 531, p. 794.

107 "I would like you to keep for yourself . . . ," Duchamp to Martins, March 19 [1950] (Taylor, *Étant donnés*, p. 417). Duchamp actually writes *pour toi* (for you), which I have taken the liberty of translating as "for yourself."

107–108 "His body was permanently shorn . . . ," Lydie Fischer Sarazin-Levassor, *A Marriage in Check: The Heart of the Bride Stripped Bare by Her Bachelor, Even*, trans. Paul Edwards (Ouphopo) (Dijon Quetigny: Les Presses du Réel, 2007), p. 74. On the shaving of Baroness Elsa's pubic hair, see Naumann, *New York Dada 1915–23* (New York: Harry N. Abrams, 1994), pp. 174, 206, 208.

110 "I realize just how much both of us are imprisoned . . . ," Duchamp to Martins, April 7 [1949] (Taylor, *Étant donnés*, p. 409).

110 Duchamp's references to the *Étant donnés* as his "Notre Dame des désirs" appear in his letters to Maria of April 3 [1950] and September 5 [1950] (Taylor, *Étant donnés*, p. 419).

110–11 "What is the situation now?" Duchamp to Martins, May 31 [1949] (Taylor, *Étant donnés*, p. 413).

111 "The simplicity of forms . . . ," Maria Martins, "Poeira da vida," in *Correio da Manhã*, November 12, 1967; in Stigger, *Maria Martins: Metamorphoses*, p. 277.

111–113 On Maria's involvement in the organization of the Bienal, see letters from Francisco Matarazzo Sobrinho to Marcel Duchamp, July 1948; Duchamp to Sobrinho, August 5, 1948; and Sobrinho to Maria Martins, September 24, 1948 (Historical Archives of the Fundação Bienal, Museu de Arte Moderna, São Paulo, Brazil).

113 "Your statues are a good illustration . . . ," Michel Tapié,

"Magic Maria Message," *Les Statues Magiques de Maria* (Paris: Galerie René Drouin, 1948); English trans. in Naumann, *Surrealist Sculpture of Maria Martins*, p. 45.

113   "I like the 8th Veil a great deal . . . ," Duchamp to Martins, October 6 [1949] (Taylor, *Étant donnés*, p. 415).

115   "We do not need a Marshall Plan for Brazil . . . ," quoted in Lucia Brown, "Good Will Ambassadress Returns: Mme. Martins Still Chic, Fiery—And Charming," *Washington Post*, December 4, 1949.

116   "Criticism against modern art . . . ," Duchamp quoted in *Maria: Esculturas* (São Paulo: Museu de Arte Moderna, 1950), unpaginated.

116   "I feel totally lost . . . ," Duchamp to Martins, March 19 [1950] (Taylor, *Étant donnés*, p. 417).

116   "You are condemned and damned . . . ," Duchamp to Martins, February 12 [1950] (Taylor, *Étant donnés*, p. 419).

116   "There is no ersatz love . . . ," Duchamp to Martins, May 13 [1951?] (Taylor, *Étant donnés*, p. 421).

117   All letters from Duchamp to Martins dating from 1951 (Taylor, *Étant donnés*, p. 423).

121   The German art historian is Dieter Daniels; see his *Duchamp und die anderen: Der Modelfall einer kunstlerischen Wirkungsgeshichte in der Moderne* (Cologne: DuMont, 1992), p. 285.

124   For critics describing the two erotic objects, see Margaret Breuning, "Pots, Pranks and Painting," *Art Digest,* December 15, 1953, p. 14; Stuart Preston, "Diverse Faces: Moderns in Wide Variety," *New York Times*, December 20, 1953; and James Fitzsimmons, "Art," *Arts & Decoration,* February 1953, p. 31.

126   "We still have it on our table . . . ," Pierre Cabanne, *Dialogues with Marcel Duchamp*, trans. Ronald Padgett (New York: Viking Press, 1971), p. 88. Although the interview was first published in French in 1967 (Paris: Editions Pierre Belfond), it actually took place in 1966 (as acknowledged in the interview itself, English ed., pp. 80, 91).

127   "Growing old . . . ," Duchamp to Arensberg, January 23, 1954 (Arensberg Archives, Philadelphia Museum of Art), in Naumann and Hector Obalk, eds., *Affectionately, Marcel: The Selected Correspondence of Marcel Duchamp* (Ghent: Ludion Press, 2000), p. 336. Duchamp wrote these words in French: "En vieillissant, l'ermite se fait diable."

128　"I don't give it a personal definition . . . ," Cabanne, *Dialogues with Duchamp*, p. 88.

128　"Where did you get that?" Hamilton's recollection of Duchamp's reaction is recorded in an interview with Calvin Tomkins; quoted in Tomkins, *Duchamp*, p. 437.

129　"No. It's not a cast . . . ," interview in Richard Hamilton's studio with R. B. Kitaj, Richard Hamilton, Robert Melville, and David Sylvester, London, June 19, 1966; transcript, The Arts Council of Great Britain, London, pp. 23–24.

129–30　Duchamp's last meeting with Maria is documented in "Duchamp e Heitor Coutinho," *Correio da Manha* (Rio de Janeiro), March 10, 1966 (clipping preserved in the Artists' Files, Museum of Modern Art, São Paulo). Also see Wesley Duke Lee, "Duchamp," in *Wesley Duke Lee*, 2nd ed. (São Paulo: Instituto Brasileiro de Arte e Cultura, 1992), pp. 12–14. (This reference was drawn to my attention and translated for me by Oswaldo Costa.)

130　Maria said that she saw the *Étant donnés* completed in a letter to Evan Turner, director of the Philadelphia Museum, April 15, 1969; cited in Taylor, *Étant donnés*, p. 131.

130　The scholar who speculated that Maria might have been present when Duchamp signed the work is Beth Gates Warren, in Warren and Marie Difilippantonio, "Maria Martins," in *Julien Levy: The Man, His Gallery, The Legacy* (Jean and Julien Levy Foundation for the Arts / New York: Artbook D.A.P., 2023), p. 2145.

132–33　On the damage sustained by *Yara*, see Taylor, *"Don't Forget I Come from the Tropics,"* p. 82.

133　On Johns's description of the *Étant donnés*, see Calvin Tomkins, *Off the Wall: Robert Rauschenberg and the Art World of Our Time* (Garden City, NY: Doubleday, 1980), p. 276. For an account of the public reaction to the work, see Taylor, *Étant donnés*, pp. 173–77.

133　"The study is close to the final work . . . ," d'Harnoncourt and Hopps, *"Étant donnés: 1° la chute d'eau / 2° le gaz d'éclairage*: Reflections on a New Work by Marcel Duchamp," *Philadelphia Museum of Art Bulletin 64*, nos. 299–300 (April–June 1969 and July–September 1969), p. 35.

136　On the *Female Fig Leaf* having been cast from a fragment, see Melissa S. Meighan, "A Technical Discussion of the Figure in Marcel Duchamp's *Étant donnés*," in Michael Taylor, ed., *Marcel Duchamp: Étant donnés* (Philadelphia Museum of Art, 2009), figs. B.26, B.27a–b, pp. 254–55.

136   The full quote from Duchamp reads: "I want to grasp things with the mind the way the penis is grasped by the vagina." As told to Lawrence D. Steefel, *The Position of Duchamp's Glass in the Development of His Art* (New York: Garland, 1977), p. 312.

136   That Duchamp envisioned the posthumous display of his *Étant donnés* as akin to a final move in a game of chess is given in Naumann, *Marcel Duchamp: The Art of Chess* (New York: Readymade Press, 2009), pp. 33–34.

137   Pedro Manuel is quoted in Ramos, *Maria Martins*, p. 191.

140   "Just as *Étant donnés* summarizes Duchamp's oeuvre . . . ," Ramos, "Étant donnés and Canto da noite: a parallel," in *Maria Martins*, pp. 248–52. Ramos describes what she sees as the figure's mouth as follows: "Focusing on the head of this extravagant being, the viewer will perceive a devouring mouth, its tongue near the lower lip" (p. 249). She sees the woman's gender in another part of the sculpture: "It is also possible to identify, in what would be the junction of the legs, the inward curving form that recalls the female genital organs" (p. 249).

140   "great thinkers and great artists . . . ," quoted in Ramos, *Maria Martins: Escultora dos Trópicos*, p. 182.

140   "For the true artist . . . ," Maria Martins, *Nietzsche: Deuses Malditos I* (Rio de Janeiro: Civilização Brasileira, 1965), p. xi; cited and translated in Veronica Stigger, "Writings by Maria Martins: 1958–65," in Cosac, *Maria*, p. 265.

140   "Death, after all . . . ," quoted in Clarice Lispector, "Diálogos possiveis: Maria Martins: e juventude tem sempre razão," *Manchete* (Rio de Janeiro), December 21, 1968, year 16, p. 870; partially quoted in Ramos, *Maria*, p. 238.

141   "I have a gypsy soul . . . ," from an interview published in *O Jornal* (Rio de Janeiro), November 9, 1956; cited by Raúl Antelo, *Maria con Marcel: Duchamp en los Trópicos* (Buenos Aires: Siglo XXI Editores Argentina, 2006), p. 160. I am grateful to Anna Israel for having drawn my attention to this citation.

141   "Besides, it's always the others who die," *Marcel Duchamp, Notes*, Paul Matisse, ed., n. 256. The date of this note is unknown, although it appears on the same sheet of paper as his ideas for a waistcoat to be made for Teeny, Peret, Sally, and Betty, which date from 1957–61 (Schwarz, *Complete Works*, cat. 554).

144–45   To my knowledge, the only author to suggest that the two

early drawings of Maria's body were the result of a collaboration was Barbara Probst Solomon, "Marcel Duchamp,
the Pesky Body Thing, and *Étant donnés*," in Solomon, ed.,
The Reading Room 4 (New York: Great Marsh Press, 2002),
p. 74. Unfortunately, at the time of her writing, Solomon
seemed unaware of my prior article on this subject, where
I argued that Duchamp was profoundly influenced by the
sculpture of Maria Martins (Naumann, "Marcel & Maria,"
Art in America 89, no. 4 [April 2001], pp. 98–111, 157).

145   Duchamp uses the word *notre* in two letters to Martins,
one written on April 3 [1950] and another on September 5
[1950], Taylor, *Étant donnés*, pp. 417, 419.

146   The first to link the *Étant donnés* to the Black Dahlia
Murder Case was the French scholar Jean-Michel Rabaté,
"Étant donnés: 1° L'art, 2° le crime; Duchamp criminal de
l'avant-garde," *Interfaces* (Paris and Worcester, MA), no.
14 (June 1998), pp. 113–30. See also Mark Nelson and Sara
Bayliss, *Exquisite Corpse: Surrealism and the Black Dahlia
Murder* (New York Bullfinch Press, 2008). The writings of
these authors and others have been evaluated and challenged in Taylor, *Étant donnés*, pp. 194–196.

147   "The idea of repeating myself . . . ," from an interview with
Georges Charbonnier, in *Entretiens avec Marcel Duchamp*,
André Gervais, ed. (Marseille: André Dimanche, 1994), p.
18. The original interview was conducted in Paris for Radio
Française on December 9, 1960 (see Cooper and Caumont,
"Ephemerides," December 9, 1960).

CHRONOLOGY

1942

Spring: Maria Martins takes a studio in New York at 471 Park Avenue (corner of 58th Street; Fig. 10) and begins preparing for her first solo show in New York at the Valentine Gallery on 57th Street.

May 11–May 30: Sculptures by Maria, Valentine Gallery, New York. The Metropolitan Museum of Art purchases *St. Francis,* and shortly thereafter *Yara* (Fig. 6) is purchased by the Philadelphia Museum of Art.

June 25: Duchamp arrives in New York. He first stays as a guest in the home of Robert Parker at 1 Gracie Square.

July 22: While they are on vacation for the summer, Duchamp stays in the home of Peggy Guggenheim and Max Ernst at 440 East 51st Street.

September 7: Article appears in *Time* magazine reporting on Duchamp's activities in New York since his arrival, particularly on his "Monograph," as they refer to the *Boîte-en-valise.* Reproduced is a photograph of the artist in Peggy Guggenheim's apartment displaying the valise (Fig. 17).

October 2: Duchamp sublets a room from Stefi and Frederick Kiesler at 56 Seventh Avenue; it has its own bathroom and private entrance on the twentieth floor of the building. This will remain his residence for one year.

October 30: Peggy Guggenheim's Art of This Century Gallery opens at 30 West 57th Street. Featured in the show is an example of Duchamp's *Boîte-en-valise* (Fig. 12), parts of which were available for view in a structure designed by Frederick Kiesler (Fig. 13).

1943

January 6, 1943: After nearly six months of perilous travel, Mary Reynolds arrives in New York. She takes an apartment at 73 Perry Street in Greenwich Village, a short walk from the building where Duchamp is living.

March 23–April 10: Maria: New Sculptures (a combined exhibition with *Mondrian: New Paintings*), Valentine Gallery, New York. Maria is represented by eight "Amazonia" figures, and the exhibition is accompanied by a book written by Maria and entitled *Amazonia* (Fig. 3). Most of the sculptures are sold. Duchamp and Maria likely meet at the opening of this exhibition.

March 28: Review of Maria's show by Edward Alden Jewell appears in the *New York Times*.

April 1: Article on Maria entitled "Madame Carlos Martins" appears in *Vogue*.

May 12: At the close of Maria's exhibition, she acquires Mondrian's *Broadway Boogie Woogie* for $800 (which officially enters into the collection of the Museum of Modern Art, New York, on this date).

May 12: Mary Reynolds and Duchamp have dinner with Stefi and Frederick Kiesler and Howard Putzel.

Maria, through the introduction of André Breton and Marcel Duchamp, meets various members of the Surrealist group (Fig. 7).

October: Duchamp moves from the room he sublet in Kiesler's building to a studio apartment around the corner at 210 West 14th Street; it is a fourth-floor walk-up with a shared bathroom, for which Duchamp pays a $35 monthly rent.

December 7–28: Through the Big End of the Opera Glass opens at the Julien Levy Gallery in New York. Duchamp organizes the exhibition and designs the announcement, which features the image of a Cupid though which can be seen a chessboard (Fig. 15).

1944

January: Duchamp gives Julien Levy a deluxe example of his *Boîte-en-valise* that has mounted in its lid his original assemblage

of cut cardboard with chicken wire used a year earlier for a back
cover of *VVV* magazine (March 1943), which he here inscribes *La
Fourchette du Cavalier* (The Knight's Fork; Fig. 16), a chess term.

February: A black-and-white photograph of Maria's *Macumba*
appears in the Surrealist magazine *VVV*, edited by David Hare.
It also contains a reproduction of Duchamp's *Genre Allegory*.

May 8–27: Maria: Sculptures and Sculpted Jewels, Valentine Gallery,
New York. Shows seven sculptures: (1) *Macumba*; (2) *Cobra Grande*;
(3) *Ma Chanson*; (4) *Passagarda*; (5) *Les deux sacres*; (6) *Uriapirú*;
and (7) *Le Couple*, as well as eight pieces of jewelry.

May 14: Maria's show is reviewed in the *New York Times* by Howard
Devree.

May 27: Maria's exhibition is unfavorably reviewed by the
American critic Clement Greenberg in *The Nation*, although he
notes that she is an artist with "immense talent."

July 1: A full-page black-and-white photograph of Maria's face seen
behind a glass supporting her jewelry appears in *Vogue* magazine
(Fig. 9). Duchamp is suspected as the designer of the image.

1945

Maria works on the production of new sculptures for her next
show at the Valentine Gallery, such as *Glèbe-Ailes* (Earthly Wings)
(1944; Fig. 22); *I Long Dreamed That I Was Free* (1945–46; Fig. 26);
and *Impossible* (1945–46; Fig. 23).

January 27: Maria receives a check in the amount of $15,000
from Nelson Rockefeller for sculptures he purchased from her in
the previous year.

March: Special issue of *View* magazine devoted to Duchamp.

March 21 (through May 13): Piet Mondrian opens at the Museum
of Modern Art, New York (Fig. 17). It is likely that Duchamp and
Maria see this show together. On view at the same time in the
museum is Duchamp's *Large Glass* (Fig. 19), which was borrowed
for an exhibition in 1943 called *Art in Progress*, but will remain
on display through 1946 (Fig. 18).

April: Mary Reynolds returns to Paris.

April 19–26: Window installation by Duchamp to promote André Breton's *Arcade 17* at Brentano's bookstore on Fifth Avenue is taken down because of protests from the League of Women. It is reinstalled in the window of Gotham Book Mart on West 47th Street. The installation features a headless female mannequin in a sleeveless party dress, which some think could relate to his future work on the *Étant donnés*.

Maria begins working on various versions of her *Impossible*, 1945–46; changes from one example of the sculpture to the next occur most noticeably in the articulation of the female figure's arms (Figs. 23 and 24).

June: Maria sends a copy of her *Amazonia* book to Walter Arensberg in Los Angeles, likely at the suggestion of Marcel Duchamp.

October 13: In his regular column for the *Sun*, Henry McBride mentions that jewelry by Maria is available for viewing at the Valentine Gallery.

November: "Madame Martins Is a Gifted Sculptress" appears in the magazine *Brazil*. The unnamed author claims that "she will probably always be remembered for her greatest work, the powerful figure of Christ carved in jacaranda."

Maria studies printmaking at Stanley William Hayter's Atelier 17, which, during the war years, moves from Paris to temporary quarters in the New School for Social Research in New York.

1946

Spring (?): In what is believed to be the first of his many letters to Maria, Duchamp openly announces his affection for her, declaring, "It has at last been granted to me to love you simply and purely."*

April 6: Duchamp presents Maria with a deluxe example of his *boîte-en-valise*, into the lid of which is mounted his *Paysage fautif* (Faulty Landscape; Fig. 20), made entirely out of his own seminal fluid.

*The dates given for Duchamp's letters to Maria Martins follow those provided in Michael R. Taylor, *Étant donnés*, (Philadelphia Museum of Art, 2009), pp. 405–25. How specific dates for some of the letters were determined is unknown, as the original envelopes—and thus postmarks— were not preserved.

April 23–May 25: Maria: New Sculptures, Valentine Gallery, New York. Maria shows eleven sculptures dating from 1943 through 1946, including a plaster version of *Impossible*. She also shows seven pieces of jewelry that are called in the catalogue "Sculptures in Gold." On the occasion of the exhibition, a deluxe portfolio of engravings is published.

May 6: Maria is interviewed in *Time* magazine, and she declares that "art is the underground of the world, and we will win in the end." The article is accompanied by a reproduction of the plaster version of Maria's *Impossible*.

April 28: Maria's show at the Valentine Gallery is reviewed by Edward Alden Jewell for the *New York Times*. The plaster version of *Impossible* is reproduced.

Duchamp makes his first sketch for the *Étant donnés*, a detailed drawing of the underside of Maria's foot (Fig. 34), which he later mounts into the lid of a valise and gives to his friend the Italian American artist Enrico Donati.

May 1: Duchamp boards the SS *Brazil* and sails to France; there he will spend the next eight months.

May 12: Duchamp writes to Maria telling her that he is "in a state of terrible depression."

June: Maria arrives in Paris. On June 29, she and Duchamp dine with Henri-Pierre Roché at the Côtelette, a restaurant near the Gare Saint-Lazare. It is likely at this time that he gives her a deluxe copy of his *Green Box* (Figs. 30 and 31) containing his first drawing for *The Large Glass* (Fig. 32), which he inscribes *pour Maria, enfin arivée*.

July 7: Maria returns to Washington, DC, aboard a flight with Henri-Pierre Roché.

July 29: Duchamp and Mary Reynolds embark upon a holiday in Switzerland. They stay at the French ambassador's residence in Bern; the ambassador and his wife, Henri and Hélène Hoppenot, are friends of Mary's.

August: Duchamp and Mary stay at the Hôtel Bellevue in Chexbres, recommended by Hélène Hoppenot, who stayed there as a child. Duchamp photographs the nearby waterfall (Fig. 39).

1947

January 13: Duchamp returns to New York.

April: With Duchamp's advice, Maria purchases the painting
Le Modèle Rouge (1935) from René Magritte's show at the Hugo
Gallery in New York. Duchamp later arranges for this work to be
reproduced on the cover of André Breton's *Le Surréalisme et
la peinture.* (The painting is now in the collection of the Musée
National d'Art Moderne, Paris.) He also arranges for her to
purchase the papier-mâché maquette used to make the urinal in
his *Boîte-en-valise* from Henri-Pierre Roché in Paris.

April 25: Marcel and Maria have dinner at the Café Brittany with
Roberto Matta and the Kieslers.

May 13: From the apartment of Maria Martins, Duchamp attempts
to call André Breton by phone in Paris. He is with Matta, Kiesler,
and Enrico Donati, his collaborators on the forthcoming Surrealist
exhibition in Paris. For reasons that are unknown, the call does not
go through.

May 17: In preparation for making the covers of the catalogue of
the Surrealist exhibition in Paris, Duchamp makes a plaster cast
of Maria's breast (Fig. 44). He and his collaborator Enrico Donati
decide that it would be easiest to purchase 999 foam-rubber falsies
and attach them to the cover instead. They work together to
paint the fake breasts and mount them individually on boards,
which are shipped to Paris to be affixed to each catalogue (Fig. 45).

July 7: Accompanied by Maria Martins, Duchamp calls on Stefi
Kiesler.

July 11: Duchamp writes to Maria with a detailed account of his
work on the skin of his mannequin.

July–August: Exposition Internationale du Surréalisme, Galerie Maeght,
Paris. Two sculptures by Maria are included in the exhibition:
The Road, The Shadow; Too Long, Too Narrow (Fig. 46), and *Impossible,*
which is displayed on a billiard table (Fig. 47). Duchamp is represented in the exhibition by two works, *The Green Ray* (installed by
Frederick Kiesler in accordance with Duchamp's instructions)
and *The Juggler of Gravity* (executed by Matta).

September 1–7: Duchamp participates in the New York State Chess Championship Tournament in Endicott, New York.

November 25–January 2: Maria, Julien Levy Gallery, New York. The catalogue features an important essay in French on Maria's sculpture by André Breton. Twelve sculptures are shown.

November 30: Howard Devree reviews Maria's show at the Julien Levy Gallery for the *New York Times*, which he finds a welcome departure from her earlier work, which, he says, "has given way to more clearly plastic manifestation."

December 9: Duchamp and Maria visit the Kieslers at 56 Seventh Avenue.

December 15: Maria's show at the Julien Levy Gallery is reviewed in *The Art Digest*; the unidentified author chastises the gallery for presenting the catalogue text only in French.

December: Maria serves as a model for a sketch Duchamp makes of her standing naked with one leg upraised that he inscribes: *Étant donnés: Maria, la chute d'eau et le gaz d'éclairage* (Given: Maria, the waterfall and the illuminating gas; Fig. 40). He gives this sketch to her, and it remains in her possession until the end of her life.

Duchamp makes a collage study of his *Étant donnés* figure in a landscape (Fig. 41), incorporating photographs he had taken of the waterfall in Switzerland a year earlier.

1948

Carlos Martins is named ambassador to France, and the family moves to Paris. Maria rents a studio at the Villa d'Alesia, across the street from Brancusi's studio. The two sculptors become close friends and enjoy many meals together cooked by Brancusi in his studio. After a few months, Maria moves to a studio on the rue de l'Université owned by the Galerie René Drouin, where her next show is planned.

April 1: In a letter to Henri-Pierre Roché, Duchamp tells him that Maria, who is now back in Brazil, "has had pneumonia followed by pleurisy, but has recovered quite quickly."

May: Maria returns to New York, presumably to close up her apartment and studio for her move to Paris. She departs New York on July 9.

May 23: Duchamp and Maria, together with Enrico and Claire Donati and Frederick Kiesler, visit the home of Kay Sage and Yves Tanguy in Woodbury, Connecticut (Fig. 43). They play boules on the lawn behind the house.

July 7: Duchamp and Maria go out to dinner with Yves Tanguy, Kay Sage, and Frederick Kiesler at the Terrace Restaurant in New York.

July 17: Duchamp writes to Maria in Paris, asking her to relay "the funny little stories that will happen to her in *gay Paree*."

August 5: Duchamp sells his *Coffee Mill*—which he painted for his brother's kitchen in 1911 but considers among his most important works—to Maria. He writes to her on this day saying, "It is fortunate that we have this little business of the *Coffee Mill* to rekindle our spirits, for I can feel myself 'dissolving' in the worst sense of the word."

August: Mary Reynolds visits New York, staying in Virgil Thomson's suite in the Chelsea Hotel. She stays there until August 21st and then goes to visit her brother in Chicago. She returns to New York in September but returns to Paris at the beginning of November.

September 6: Duchamp writes to Maria during a break from a chess tournament in which he is participating in Endicott, New York. He tells her that when he gets back to New York, he will continue his progress on "my dry skin under its steel rods," and reports: "I have even started to draw the woman. (In pencil.)"

October 12: In a letter to Maria, Duchamp writes, "How I would like to breathe with you."

October–November: Maria's first solo exhibition in Paris at the Galerie René Drouin. To mark the occasion, the gallery publishes *Les Statues Magiques de Maria*, the first major book on the artist's work, which contains essays by André Breton (the same one included in the Julien Levy Gallery catalogue of 1947) and the French art critic Michael Tapié.

Marcel Duchamp draws *Réflection à main*, which he will mount into the lid of a *Boîte-en-valise* that he gives to the Hoppenots in 1949 (Fig. 51).

1949

April 7: Duchamp writes to Maria that friends want to keep them "in a cage." He says that he spends a lot of time trying to figure out a way to escape but warns her that they must not allow themselves to "be trapped by their 'environment.'" He recommends she seek solace in her sculpture, whereas he will continue work on "my woman with open pussy."

May 6: Duchamp writes to Maria with his suggestion of a title for one of her sculptures, for which she has sent a sketch. He suggests "AMOUR POUR COMBIEN D'AUTANT MIEUX" (LOVE FOR HOW MANY SO MUCH THE BETTER).

May 24: Duchamp writes to Maria that he "started to dream about number 471," which was Maria's address on Park Avenue, where, he says "we had our best time, and to relive them will be joy redoubled."

May 31: Duchamp writes a long letter to Maria reporting on his progress on the mannequin in his studio: "But our woman is finished and goes to the molder's the day after tomorrow. I intend to work on the plaster cast a great deal because I can't see anything more to do with the plasteline." He ends by telling her that he is "profoundly sad" that their days of being together are decreasing, "fading away," as he says, "without any of our dreams coming true."

Duchamp finishes a painted leather over plaster relief study for the *Étant donnés* (Fig. 49) that he gives to Maria, inscribing on the verso: *Cette dame appartient à Maria Martins / avec toutes mes affections / Marcel Duchamp 1948–49* (This lady is owned by Maria Martins / with all my affection / Marcel Duchamp 1948–49).

June 6: Duchamp writes to Maria to tell her that he is upset with Alfred Barr for having told his wife about "our 'skin'," referring to the mannequin for his *Étant donnés*, which, apparently, he showed Barr on a visit to his studio.

June 30: In another long letter to Maria, Duchamp updates her on his progress on the *Étant donnés*: "I am back to working 8 hours a day, retouching the plaster cast, i.e., redoing it completely."

October 6: Duchamp writes to Maria that he has received a copy of the catalogue for her exhibition at Galerie Drouin. He says that he especially likes her *Eighth Veil* (Fig. 52) but cannot see the head clearly in reproduction, and asks her to send other photos.

November: Carlos Martins retires from diplomatic service. The family departs from Paris and returns home to São Paulo, where Maria prepares for her first major exhibition in Brazil.

December 4: An article in the *Washington Post* announces Mme. Martins is returning to her native Brazil. "We do not need a Marshall Plan for Brazil," she tells a journalist. "But we would like a greater sharing of ideas and art with our neighbors."

1950

MARIA: Esculturas opens at the Museu de Arte Moderna in São Paulo. Thirty-six sculptures are shown, which, according to the exhibition checklist, range in date from 1934 through 1950. The accompanying catalogue contains essays and statements by Duchamp, Henry McBride, Breton, Tapié, Amédée Ozenfant, Christian Zervos, and Santa Rosa.

March 19: Duchamp writes to Maria that his isolation from her is painful and provides yet another report on his progress in painting the skin of the mannequin in his studio.

April 3: Duchamp receives two letters from Maria that arrive at around the same time, both expressing "total despair" over their situation. "I am impatient for you to be here to talk about the situation in more detail," he writes in response. In a postscript he adds: "Our Lady of Desire is now flesh-pink. I am struggling against an overly fondant candy color."

September 5: Duchamp again writes to Maria about his mannequin, which this time he calls *notre gourgandine* (our hussy), saying that he is "still dressing her in her finery of nails and she waits patiently for her clothing of skin."

September 14: Duchamp departs for Paris because he is told by Frank Hubacheck, the brother of Mary Reynolds, that her health is rapidly declining. On September 30, she dies at her home on rue Hallé in Paris, Duchamp by her side. After remaining in Paris for approximately two months, Duchamp returns to New York on November 25.

Duchamp makes *Feuille de Vigne Femelle* (Female Fig Leaf) (Fig. 56), a cast from a study for the *Étant donnés*. He issues this in two editions: first in ten painted plaster casts made by Man Ray in 1951, and then in an edition of ten bronze examples with the Galerie Rive Droit in Paris in 1961.

1951

February 12: With artist and art dealer Bill Copley and his girlfriend Gloria de Herrera, Duchamp meets his old friend Man Ray, who is boarding a ship in New York to return to Paris after a ten-year so-journ in Hollywood. In the privacy of Man Ray's cabin, Duchamp gives him an example of his *Feuille de Vigne Femelle* and asks him to prepare an edition of the work in plaster.

Maria helps to organize the first Bienal Internacional de São Paulo.

Duchamp makes *Objet-Dard* (Dart Object; Fig. 55), which, in 1962, he issues in an edition of eight examples in bronze with the Galleria Schwarz, Milan.

May 13 (?): Duchamp again writes to Maria about his despair over their situation. "There is no ersatz love," he writes. "It does not exist. And by not making love we feel disgust and there is no way out. Even work is a sexual stimulant, instead of turning our atten-tion away from the physiological."

October–November: In a series of letters to Maria, Duchamp expresses his increasing frustration over their inability to remain together as lovers.

Fall: Duchamp starts dating Alexina Sattler Matisse (known to friends as "Teeny"), former wife of the art dealer Pierre Matisse.

1952

The Large Glass (Fig. 19) is bequeathed to the Philadelphia Museum of Art from the estate of Katherine S. Dreier, who dies on March 29 of this year.

1953

December: Duchamp is part of a two-person show with Francis Picabia at the Rose Fried Gallery in New York, where he shows a

Green Box, a *Boîte-en-valise*, and also two strange object-sculptures: *Objet-Dard* (Fig. 55) and *Feuille de Vigne Femelle* (Fig. 56).

1954

January 16: Duchamp and Teeny marry. As a wedding gift, he gives her his *Coin de chastité* (Wedge of Chastity; Fig. 57), the third in a trilogy of erotic objects that originate with the *Étant donnés*. He issues this object in an edition of eight examples in bronze and dental plastic in 1963 with the Galleria Schwarz, Milan.

1955–1965

In this decade, Maria continues to show her work in the São Paulo Biennale, winning the grand prize for sculpture in 1955 and 1956. She travels widely (to India and China in 1956) and begins writing and publishing books (one on China in 1958, one on politics in the Middle East in 1961, and another on Nietzsche in 1965). She is also an occasional contributor to *Correio da Manhã*, a leading newspaper in Rio.

1963

October 8–November 3: Marcel Duchamp: A Retrospective, organized by Walter Hopps, is held at the Pasadena Art Museum in California. Two of Duchamp's three erotic objects are included in the show, *Objet-Dard* (Fig. 55) and *Feuille de vigne* (Fig. 56), both borrowed from the collection of Jasper Johns.

1965

January 14–February 13: Not Seen and/or Less Seen of/by Marcel Duchamp/Rrose Sélavy 1904–1964 is held at the Cordier & Ekstrom Gallery in New York. Organized by Arne Ekstrom with Duchamp's assistance, it includes all three of the erotic objects (Figs. 55–57).

March: Maria's husband, Carlos Martins Pereira e Sousa, dies at age eighty in Rio de Janeiro from post-surgical complications.

1966

March 10: Marcel and Maria meet for the last time. They attend a tea in her honor at the home of Elba Sette Camara, wife of the Brazilian delegate to the United Nations. Later they go down to Duchamp's temporary studio in a storeroom on East 11th Street and Broadway to see the *Étant donnés*, which he signs in this year as a finished work of art (Fig. 58).

June 18-July 31: The Almost Complete Works of Marcel Duchamp, organized by the English artist Richard Hamilton, is held at the Tate Gallery in London. Included in the show is Duchamp's study for the *Étant donnés* (Fig. 49), borrowed from the collection of Maria Martins. In the exhibition it is displayed next to the three erotic objects.

June 19: Within the context of his exhibition at the Tate Gallery, Duchamp is interviewed about his work by several artists and critics; they ask about the meaning of his study for the *Étant donnés* (Fig. 49), but he refuses to talk about it, dismissing it with a single word: "Nothing."

1967

November: In what is likely the last letter of their correspondence, Duchamp writes to Maria that he has not heard from her in more than a year. "I feel much freer to do nothing now that I can invoke my 80 years to refuse any boring, shitty activities."

1968

Maria completes the large sculpture *Canto da Noite* (Song of Night; Fig. 61) for a building in Brasília. This work is thought to contain re-flections of her viewing of Duchamp's *Étant donnés* two years earlier.

October 2: Duchamp dies of heart failure at his home in Neuilly-sur-Seine, France, at the age of eighty-one.

1969

July 7: *Étant donnés: 1° la chute d'eau / 2° le gaz d'éclairage* (Given: 1° The Waterfall / 2° The Illuminating Gas; Figs. 59 and 60) is revealed to the public for the first time, installed in a room off the side of a gallery devoted to Duchamp's work at the Philadelphia Museum of Art.

1973

March 27: Maria Martins dies of heart failure at her home in Rio de Janeiro, at the age of seventy-eight.

ACKNOWLEDGMENTS

This book began as the text for a proposed catalogue that never materialized. During the summer of 2023, I was invited by Amalia Dayan and her colleague Victoria Gelfand-Magalhaes to organize an exhibition for their gallery, Lévy Gorvy Dayan (LGD), on the relationship between Marcel Duchamp and Maria Martins. At the time, they were offering a sculpture by the artist through their gallery and wished to give the work a proper context. Moreover, they thought this would be a suitable inaugural show for their new space in London, in the former Empress Club, a women's social club whose opening had been attended by Queen Victoria. They approached me because I had written on the subject of Duchamp and Martins, and they thought I would be the most qualified person to curate the sort of exhibition they had in mind.

At first I was hesitant, as I had published so much about the two artists already and presumed that I might not have anything more to say. But as I gave the project more thought, I realized that much of what I had written before had appeared in only fragmentary form: a catalogue text on Maria's surrealist sculpture for the André Emmerich Gallery in 1998, and two articles in *Art in America* (1993 and 2001). Besides, those writings were now more than twenty years old, and much had been published about both artists since—information that would be interesting, I thought, if integrated into my own work, essentially updating what I had written before but presenting it in a more detailed and focused way. I had earlier speculated that the direction of influence usually assumed when considering the work of Duchamp—going from him to virtually every artist who came in contact with his work—might, in the case of Maria Martins, have gone in the other direction, that is to say, from her to him. That might very well have been considered anathema by most Duchamp scholars, but over the years I had become increasingly determined to prove it actually occurred.

I am grateful to Amalia and Victoria for having encouraged me to reconsider this subject, even though the exhibition never took place due to the inability to secure critical museum loans. (A more modest show devoted to the work of Maria alone is planned for the not-too-distant future.) I would like to thank Anna Israel for having helped me with the Spanish and Portuguese publications, and especially Graça Ramos, whose book on Maria was indispensable to my writings, and who helped serve as a liaison in securing various photographs, particularly of Maria's *Canto da noite* in Brasília (where Ramos lives). I am especially indebted to my wife, Marie T. Keller, who is the first reader of anything I write, and whose careful editorial eye catches most of the typos and misspellings that would be embarrassing if left unnoticed and retained. Dana Martin, who initially laid this book out for me, was unfailingly patient in making my many changes to the manuscript, and for her time and tolerance I am deeply appreciative. I am also grateful to Carlos Martins Ceglia and Ignez Ceglia Simoes, the children of Nora Lobo (daughter of Maria Martins), who granted permission for me to reproduce the works by Maria Martins in this book. They were both very supportive of my project and helped me in many ways. I wish to thank Michael Steger from Janklow & Nesbit Associates for having read an initial draft of my text; the comments he made inspired my writing of the postscript. Above all, I want to thank the noted Duchamp scholar Michael R. Taylor, whose writings on Duchamp and Martins were indispensable to mine, and who read the manuscript for this book and offered many helpful suggestions to improve its content.

Finally, I wish to thank Antoine Monnier, and Séverine Gossart, directors of the Association Marcel Duchamp in Paris, who welcomed my reinvestigation of this subject. Antoine referred to my desire to write this book as an item "on my bucket list." I never thought of it that way, but he was right: in the nearly five decades that I have devoted to writing on Duchamp's art and life, I would never have been fully satisfied had I not given this subject the attention it deserves. Luckily, there was still time for me to do that, and I am grateful to Antoine for reminding me of that fact and for giving me permission to reproduce the works by Marcel Duchamp that grace the pages of the present publication.

F.N.

INDEX

ABOUT THE AUTHOR

Francis M. Naumann, MFA, PhD, is an art historian, curator, and former art dealer, specializing in the art of the Dada and Surrealist periods. He is author of numerous articles and exhibition catalogues, including *New York Dada 1915–25* (Harry N. Abrams, 1994), considered to be the definitive history of the movement. In 1998, he wrote the catalogue *Maria: The Surrealist Sculpture of Maria Martins* for an exhibition at the Emmerich Gallery in New York. He has also written several articles and books on Marcel Duchamp, including *Marcel Duchamp: The Art of Making Art in the Age of Mechanical Reproduction* (1999), and coedited *Affectionately Marcel: The Selected Correspondence of Marcel Duchamp* (2000). His articles on the artist were collected in *The Recurrent, Haunting Ghost: Essays on the Art, Life and Legacy of Marcel Duchamp* (2012). He lives with his wife (Marie T. Keller) and dogs (Willy and Benny) in Yorktown Heights, New York.